The Light Beyond

A Study of Hawthorne's Theology

The Light Beyond

by Reverend Leonard J. Fick

The Newman Press • Westminster, Maryland
1955

First published, 1955

Nihil obstat: Francis J. Schwendeman, S.T.D.
Censor Librorum
Imprimatur: ✠ Michael J. Ready, D.D.
Bishop of Columbus
July 22, 1955

To Mother Alphonsa

Foundress of the Servants for the Relief of Incurable Cancer

The Rose of All the Hawthornes

Preface

Mere literal meanings and logical exposition will not suffice to transmit ineffable truth. Of this fact Nathaniel Hawthorne was well aware. Yet he needed a set of theological concepts which might serve him as the framework, the enveloping action, for his allegorical and symbolic presentations of moral drama. Such a set of concepts he found in the Puritan theology.

This is not to say that he blindly accepted the entire structure of Puritan theology and Puritan polity. Highly individualistic in his religious temperament and approach, he cherished his freedom from denominational ties. Understandably, therefore, his probing into the eternal verities led him at times to resurrect dogmas which his New England forbears had buried beneath the rigid formalism of a legalized religion; at other times, his deeply personal sense of human values constrained him to adopt the vantage point of those who had, unwittingly perhaps, transformed the pristine piety of Plymouth Rock and Massachusetts Bay into a diluted moralism that bore little resemblance to the staunch Puritanism of an earlier day.

In view of his significant departures from that Puritanism with which the name of Nathaniel Hawthorne has been all too easily associated, the present study sets itself the task of establishing, in some detail, the initial dogmatic concepts which give coherence and meaning to Hawthorne's fictional representations of life.

2

The method adopted for this study is sufficiently outlined in the introduction. Here it need only be said that the term *theology,* as it is used in this work, includes both Hawthorne's philosophical faith (theodicy) and his revealed faith (theology properly so-called). Nor has it been deemed advisable, in view of the static character of his theological thinking, to weigh the evidence chronologically: an editorial in *The American Magazine of Useful and Entertaining Knowledge,* composed in 1836, is considered as valid a determinant of his beliefs as an entry in *The French and Italian Notebooks,* written more than a score of years later. In fact, a careful check warrants the conclusion that in no instance is the record of any seminal belief of his to be derived exclusively from evidence lodged in any one text or in any combination of texts from his earlier works, fictional or non-fictional.

Finally, no effort has been made explicitly to show which truths are most frequently embodied in his fiction, or which concepts are most ideally suited to provide him with the framework for his best work. These are separate problems and, of course, highly legitimate areas of investigation; but they do not fall within the compass of this work.

3

I am sincerely grateful to the Most Reverend Amleto Giovanni Cicognani, D.D., the Apostolic Delegate to the United States, who, in appointing me to the faculty of the Pontifical College Josephinum, Worthington, Ohio, provided the milieu conducive to a study such as this.

Likewise, with a deep sense of gratitude, I express my appreciation to Professor William Charvat, of the Ohio

State University, who first called attention to the need for a work of this kind, and whose continued interest and guidance over a period of years provided far more than the usual encouragement; to Professor Milton O. Percival, whose deep understanding of men like Blake and Emerson adequately counter-balanced my ingrained tendency to reject everything that could not be submitted to logical demonstration. Finally, I wish to acknowledge a debt of appreciation to Yale's Dr. Norman Holmes Pearson, who twice welcomed me to New Haven, discussed Hawthorne with me over "the tables down at Mory's," and made accessible his transcripts of *The French and Italian Notebooks,* the Hawthorne Letters, and the Ada Shepard Letters.

NOTE

All references to Hawthorne's writings are to be found in the respective volumes of *The Complete Works of Nathaniel Hawthorne,* with Introductory Notes by George Parsons Lathrop (Riverside Edition, Boston and New York, 1883, 12 vols.). Citations of this edition are incorporated directly into the text of the work; when the immediate source of the quotation is sufficiently clear from the context, the reference is made to volume and page alone; when the context provides no clue, obvious abbreviations of the individual works precede the volume-and-page reference—thus, *SL* (*The Scarlet Letter*), *HSG* (*The House of the Seven Gables*), *BR* (*The Blithedale Romance*), *MF* (*The Marble Faun*).

The text of every letter quoted in this study is from the typescript copy of the collection assembled for the forthcoming edition of Hawthorne's letters, under the editorship of Norman Holmes Pearson, Randall Stewart, Stanley T. Williams, and Manning Hawthorne.

Quotations from the Hawthorne notebooks are foot-noted in short-title fashion:

The American Notebooks
Stewart, Randall, ed. *The American Notebooks by Nathaniel Hawthorne.* New Haven: Yale University Press, 1932.

The English Notebooks
Stewart, Randall, ed. *The English Notebooks by Nathaniel Hawthorne.* New York and London: Modern Language Association of America and Oxford University Press, 1941.

The French and Italian Notebooks
Pearson, Norman Holmes, ed. *The French and Italian Notebooks by Nathaniel Hawthorne,* 3 Volumes. Unpublished. Yale University Library, 1941.

Passages from the American Note-Books is employed only for those portions of Hawthorne's journals not included in Professor Stewart's edition; the page reference in that case is to Volume IX of the Riverside Edition.

Acknowledgments

Thanks are due to the following for permission
to quote copyrighted material:

Appleton-Century-Crofts, Inc., New York, for *The Phi-losophy of Religion* by Fulton J. Sheen, copyright, 1948,
by Fulton J. Sheen.

Benziger Brothers, Inc., New York, for *A Manual of
Moral Theology* by Thomas Slater, S.J.

Harvard University Press, Cambridge, Massachusetts,
for *The New England Mind,* by Perry Miller.

Henry Holt and Company, Inc., New York, for *Piety
Versus Moralism* by Joseph Haroutunian.

The Modern Language Association of America, New
York, for *The English Notebooks of Nathaniel Haw-thorne.*

Random House, Inc., New York, for *The Basic Writ-ings of St. Thomas Aquinas,* edited by Anton C. Pegis.

Charles Scribner's Sons, New York, for *Three Re-formers,* by Jacques Maritain.

Yale University Press, New Haven, Connecticut, for
The American Notebooks of Nathaniel Hawthorne.

Contents

Introduction

The literal dogmatic beliefs of a St. Augustine
or a Kierkegaard are comparatively easy to
discern. This is not to say, of course, that their beliefs
can be reduced to certain definitive categories, into one
of which every single tenet of theirs can be readily
pigeonholed: for there is never absent the possibility
either of inherent contradiction in or of gradual accre-
tion to the sum of any man's theological beliefs at any
given time of his life. In either case, however, it is possible definitely to assess the contradiction or to chart the
various stages of growth, and this for the very simple
reason that such thinkers as St. Augustine and Kierkegaard have specifically recorded their dogmatic beliefs;
to be quite obvious, they have stated in effect, "This is
what I believe" or "This is what I have always held to
be true."

Now it is at once evident that there can be no question
of invoking a similar mode of procedure in determining
the dogmatic tenets of Nathaniel Hawthorne. For as a
novelist, Hawthorne legitimately availed himself of the
privilege "of imaginatively projecting states of mind,
[thus] giving experimental fulfillments to what in the man
[*sc*. the author] are but hints and implications." [1] The
statements of each character a novelist creates, therefore, may be variously interpreted: they may represent
the actual beliefs of the author; they may represent beliefs
with which the author is in sharp disagreement; they may
represent insights which the author has, and of which he

may or may not be absolutely convinced, but which the prevailing milieu of orthodoxy or heterodoxy prevents him from avowing openly; or, finally, they may be nothing more than statements fulfilling the reasonable demands of the plot for verisimilitude.

Confronted by this variety of mutually irreconcilable possibles, one is tempted simply to deny the criteriological value of novels as indicative of an author's belief. While this solution to the problem would materially restrict the area of investigation, it would, at least in the case of Hawthorne, result in a gross oversimplification. Nathaniel Hawthorne, in point of fact, insisted that anyone who would know the real Hawthorne must find him in his tales and romances. Addressing himself to Horatio Bridge, in the preface to *The Snow Image* volume, he made it quite clear that

These things [introductions to novels, prefaces, *etc.*] hide the man, instead of displaying him. You must make quite another kind of inquest, and look through the whole range of his fictitious characters, good and evil, in order to detect any of his essential traits (III, 386).

This outright admission of a superior evidential value attributable to the novels finds corroboration in the statement of his sister-in-law, Elizabeth Peabody, who wrote to Bridge on June 4, 1887, concerning a letter in which Hawthorne made some generalizing "off-the-cuff" remarks about the folly of the Civil War. Miss Peabody admitted that the letter [dated July 20, 1863] had been written to her, adding that it "ought to have been destroyed as soon as read as he always wanted his letters to be, for like his private journal, they were always written from the mood of the moment & were really never to be considered as expressing his mature thought—"

By implication, then, since neither the letters nor the journals express his mature thought, the novels and tales do and must express it. It is not clear, of course, whether the pertinent portion of the Peabody letter is an indirect quotation of a statement made by Hawthorne, or whether it expresses merely a personal opinion of one who was, for many years, closely associated with Hawthorne. Should the latter be the case, Miss Peabody's statement, made under the stress of circumstances, has only a limited value.

Nevertheless, and this the more so in view of Hawthorne's repeated insistence upon the moral of his tales, it would be folly to essay an investigation into the theology of Hawthorne without taking into consideration the fictional output of the man. Novels like *The Scarlet Letter* and *The Marble Faun,* short stories like "The Minister's Black Veil" and "Ethan Brand"—these do provide a fabric from which to derive their author's theological tenets. But just how is one to use them? What is their precise value? For example, can this sentence from "Egotism; or, the Bosom Serpent" be adduced to prove Hawthorne's belief in a New Testament God of Love rather than in an Old Testament God of Wrath?

Not merely the eye of man was a horror to him; not merely the light of a friend's countenance; but even the blessed sunshine, likewise, which in its universal beneficence typifies the radiance of the Creator's face, expressing his love for all the creatures of his hand (II, 307).

More difficult still, to what extent do the statements of individual characters represent the beliefs and insights of Hawthorne? For it is quite clear that Hawthorne cannot subscribe to every statement made by all his characters; likewise, it must be abundantly clear that the practice of discovering, more or less intuitively, a pattern of belief, and then confirming that pattern by quotations from the man's novels, quotations chosen utterly without reference to the time or place or character of the persons speaking—such a practice leaves a great deal to be desired, is, in fact, a vicious circle. Yet, if the novels are to contribute anything to this study, some principles must be ascertained, in the light of which one can justifiably use the tales and short stories as evidence of an author's beliefs. In the case of Hawthorne, such principles may well be these.

1. The statement of a character in a novel may be said to embody the actual belief of the writer, if it substantially coincides with a statement made in that same author's non-fictional works [notebooks, letters, autobiographies].

As a principle, this may seem to be nothing but a pretentious formulation of the obvious; yet it is subject both to a restriction and to an extension which are not quite so obvious. The restriction is this: the fact that a character in the novel voices the sentiments of an author on one occasion does not justify the reader in assuming that everything spoken by that character represents the author's opinion. Obviously each separate statement must be interpreted in the light of information culled from non-fictional works. However—and this is the extension noted above—the character in the novel may easily be the vehicle whereby an author formulates his opinion in greater detail, always provided the substance of the statement can be shown, again from non-fictional sources, to embody the actual belief, opinion, or sentiment of the author. It is, of course, only in the latter case that this principle has any value for an examination into Hawthorne's theology.

By way of illustration, and with specific reference to Hawthorne, I submit two texts, the first from *The French and Italian Notebooks,* the other from *The Marble Faun.*

The relation between the confessor and his penitent might, and ought to be, one of great tenderness and beauty; and the more I see of the Catholic church, the more I wonder at the exuberance with which it responds to the demands of human infirmity. If its ministers were themselves a little more than human, they might fulfill their office, and supply all that men need.[2]

In *The Marble Faun,* now, the author, speaking through the thought stream of Hilda, writes:

There is no one want or weakness of human nature for which Catholicism will own itself without a remedy . . .

To do it justice, Catholicism is such a miracle of fitness for its own ends . . . that it is difficult to imagine it a contrivance of mere man. Its mighty machinery was forged and put together, not on middle earth, but either above or below. If there were but angels to work it, instead of the very different class of engineers who now manage its cranks and safety-valves, the system would soon vindicate the dignity and holiness of its origin (VI, 392 f.).

Substantially, these two statements voice the same opinion; in the latter, however, the passage from the novel, it will be noted that the author expresses a conviction regarding the supernatural origin of Catholicism— a "detail" not incorporated into the quotation from the *Notebooks,* yet representing, in view of the identity of context, a verifiable statement of Hawthorne's position.

A second criterion for assessing the evidential value of a statement found in the novels and tales is this:

2. Any statement logically based upon, deriving from, or conformable either to a pattern of belief or to a theory of action definitely known from non-fictional primary sources, may be said to represent the authorial position.

Again by way of exemplification, consider the problem posed by a passage from "The Celestial Railroad."

. . . . into their deserted cave another terrible giant has thrust himself, and makes it his business to seize upon honest travellers and fatten them for his table with plentiful meals of smoke, mist, moonshine, raw potatoes, and sawdust.

He is a German by birth, and is called Giant Transcendentalist; but as to his form, his features, his substance, and his nature generally, it is the chief peculiarity of this huge miscreant that neither he for himself, nor anybody for him, has ever been able to describe them. As we rushed by the cavern's mouth we caught a hasty glimpse of him, looking somewhat like an ill-proportioned figure, but considerably more like a heap of fog and duskiness. He shouted after us, but in so strange a phraseology that we knew not what he meant, nor whether to be encouraged or affrighted (II, 224).

Does this passage indicate Hawthorne's actual opinion of transcendentalism, or is it a mere fictional device to secure timeliness for and arouse interest in the story? The text itself provides no certain clue; and were this the only mention of transcendentalism in all of Hawthorne, his position in regard to transcendentalism would remain forever uncertain, unless, of course, some reliable contemporary opinion of his views on the subject were available. However, references in the notebooks and letters, and unimpeachable biographical data make it possible to say without fear of error that this passage from "The Celestial Railroad" is a true statement of Hawthorne's views. Once that is established, a detailed investigation of the passage will bring to light added information, as, for example, the reason for his opposition to transcendentalism.

2

These two principles, it will be noted, derive their criteriological character from sources external to the novels. In other words, these principles are useless in cases in which all the primary sources for determining an author's beliefs are couched exclusively in the fictional medium. But even were this the case with Hawthorne, the problem, though more difficult, would yet be soluble. For throughout Hawthorne's novels there are many and oftentimes lengthy passages of authorial advice—passages in which the author halts the story, buttonholes the reader, and states his position, clearly and unmistakably, as, for example, in this sentence from *The Marble Faun:*

Here, likewise, is seen a symbol (as apt at this moment as it was 2,000 years ago) of the Human Soul, with its choice of Innocence or Evil close at hand, in the pretty figure of the child, clasping a dove to her bosom, but assaulted by a snake (VI, 19).

There can be no reasonable doubt that in a sentence such as this Hawthorne is voicing his own views: the passage adduced is not spoken by any of the characters in the novel, nor is it in the thought stream of any of those characters. This being so, it can be adduced at least as adminicular proof of Hawthorne's position regarding the freedom of the will. Now in the tales of Hawthorne these sections of authorial comment, occurring, as they do, in quantity, unite to form a definite framework of reference; and once such a framework has been established, the second principle, previously listed, applies.

The third principle, then, is this:

3. Parenthetical passages containing what can only be authorial advice or comment may be said to state the author's position on the subject with which they deal.

A fourth and final principle may be deduced from the presence of identical or closely related themes in the major works of an author. This principle may be formulated as follows:

4. Recurrent themes—whether of problem or of solution, or both—demonstrate an author's interest in and concern for that problem, and his predilection for the solution propounded to that problem.

Obviously, Hawthorne's constant preoccupation in his novels with sin and guilt and its consequences is evidence of far more than a mere fictional or academic interest. It is evidence of a deeply rooted concern for the problems posed by the presence of sin and evil in the world; it is evidence, too, of an underlying determination to probe the mystery and the ramifications of moral evil, not necessarily, it is true, with a view to resolving the mystery, but certainly with a view to reconciling the reader to the mystery. In the absence of other evidence, which fortunately, in the case of Hawthorne, is not lacking, the validity of this principle must find its proof in the laws of human psychology: a continued preoccupation with any subject evinces an interest which must, somehow, arrive at conclusions concerning that subject. These conclusions, or reconciliations, if reducible to a pattern, may be said to represent the actual belief of the author, and this even though they find expression solely in a fictional medium.

These four principles—two of them deriving their validity from external evidence, two, from internal evidence—even if correctly applied, can never produce complete certitude. They can only engender a degree of probability. Nor do they cause every difficulty to disappear. For one thing, as Austin Warren points out,[3] no novelist need come to a decision between alternatives. "He can divide his conflicting insights between his characters"— as may well be the case, for example, when Hawthorne has Miriam, and Kenyon, too, propose what is presumably the theory of the educative value of sin. In such cases, it is proper to assume that these views were considered by the author, that he toyed with them as possible solutions. Whether he himself, not as a novelist, but as an individual, finally accepted or rejected them can be determined only by placing them into the general framework of his thought, and then deciding whether they are consistent with it or not.

Finally, it should be noted that the difficulty of arriving at Hawthorne's actual position on any matter from a study of his novels seems almost eliminated were one to adopt the theory of author-observers suggested by Amy Louise Reed.[4] According to this theory, Coverdale [in *The Blithedale Romance*], Holgrave [in *The House of the Seven Gables*], and Kenyon [in *The Marble Faun*] are actually Hawthorne. Their statements are those of Hawthorne himself and represent his true position, namely, the beliefs to which he would subscribe in a personal, non-fictional credo. Ingenious as this hypothesis is, and even possible, in view of the similarity between the self-admitted Paul Pry-ishness of Hawthorne and that of the three characters in question, and, in the case of Coverdale, the close resemblance between *The American Notebook* entries from April through October, 1841, and the first nine chapters of *The Blithedale Romance*— despite this, the author-observer theory does not do away with a very basic question: "Granted that Kenyon (or Coverdale or Holgrave) is Hawthorne, just how much of what Kenyon says is spoken to meet the purely fictional requirements of the tale, and how much of it is personally Hawthorne?" And the question is still apropos even if one adopts the position that Hawthorne wrote his novels for no other purpose than to propagandize his views. Unless, therefore, one were to hold the untenable view that everything Kenyon says is Hawthorne speaking as a person, the author-observer hypothesis depends for its value on the principles already set forth. And it is in the light of these principles, here briefly indicated, that the novels and tales of Hawthorne, conjointly with other primary sources, will be used in this investigation into the theology of Nathaniel Hawthorne.

NOTES

[1] Austin Warren, *Rage for Order* (Chicago: The University of Chicago Press, 1948), p. 89.

[2] *The French and Italian Notebooks,* II, 114.

[3] Warren, *op. cit.,* p. 89.

[4] Amy Louise Reed, "Self-Portraiture in the Work of Nathaniel Hawthorne," *Studies in Philology,* XXIII (January, 1926), 40-54.

The Light Beyond

In the Last Judgment the scene . . . lies in the upper sky, the blue of which glows through betwixt the groups of naked figures; and above sits Jesus, not looking in the least like the Savior of the world, but with uplifted arm denouncing eternal misery on those whom he came to save. I fear I am myself among the wicked, for I found myself inevitably taking their part, and asking for at least a little pity, some few regrets, and not such a stern denunciatory spirit on the part of Him who had thought us worth dying for. . . . It would be a very terrible picture to one who should really see Jesus, the Savior, in that inexorable Judge; but it seems to me very undesirable that he should ever be represented in that aspect, when it is so essential to our religion to believe him infinitely kinder and better towards us than we deserve.

—*The French and Italian Notebooks,* II, 254 f.

I *God*

In sharp contrast to the ever increasing number of emancipated Puritans among whom he lived out his sixty and more years, Nathaniel Hawthorne retained his interest in the complex foliations of the inward life. On all sides of him, the spiritual descendants of the Mather-Edwards dynasty were losing interest in the phenomena of the inner life. Instead, they adopted an approach successfully canonized by Ben Franklin[1] and concerned themselves chiefly with the material problems of an external world.

Not so Nathaniel Hawthorne. His major interest was still the observation and study of the human soul. From the facts of consciousness he sought to build the structure of reality—not, indeed, from those facts of consciousness exclusively peculiar to himself, but from such as were at once common to himself and to all mankind. Writing to Sophia Peabody on February 27, 1842, he specifically alluded to this element of commonality.

And when people think that I am pouring myself out in a tale or essay, I am merely telling what is common to human nature, not what is peculiar to myself. I sympathize with them—not they with me.

Nine years later, in his prefatory remarks to *The Snow Image* volume, he referred to the charge of egotism brought against him because of the "preliminary talk" with which he was wont to introduce his tales.

And, as for egotism, a person, who has been burrowing, to his utmost ability, into the depths of our common nature, for the purposes of psychological romance,—and who pursues his researches in that dusky region, as he needs must, as well by the tact of his sympathy as by the light of observation,—will smile at incurring such an imputation . . . (III, 386).

Psychological observation remained for him, as for the Puritans before him, and for St. Augustine before them, the necessary antechamber to metaphysics. In fact, if one would note, at the very outset, the type of mind from which proceeds the theology of Hawthorne, one can with profit institute a preliminary general comparison between the New England novelist and the "patron saint" of Puritanism.[2]

To a certain extent, Augustine's theology was "a theology of experience." This is not to say that God—to name but one truth among many—had no reality for him save as an object of experience or as a fact of consciousness. But it does mean that, in his capacity as theologian, he in the first instance derived the objects of his thought from his own inward life, and brought all problems which imposed themselves from without into relation with himself. Nor was he too concerned with correlating his various views, consonant though they may have been, into a higher synthesis; he was content to let them lie about in a somewhat haphazard unconnected fashion, in a relation of mere juxtaposition one to another.

In all this, of course, Augustine is a far cry from Thomas Aquinas. "To the mind of St. Thomas, the subject thinking, the theologian, is utterly subordinate to the object thought, to the sublime reality of revealed truth."[3] St. Thomas's philosophical and theological structure, in which there is nothing haphazard or unrelated, derives its coldness and rigidity from his fast exclusion of all subjectivity. Hence, its validity is in no way dependent upon either the person or the milieu of the man who gave scholasticism its most perfect expression.

It is at once evident, from what has been said, that Hawthorne's approach to metaphysics is Augustinian rather than Thomistic. Not only was his the empirical and psychological habit of mind invariably associated with Augustine, but, like Augustine, who first used the term *docta ignorantia* (learned ignorance),[4] he realized the limitations of human knowledge. His device of multiple choice, of alternative possibilities, his penchant for dividing his insights among his several characters are, as will be seen, his admission of the imperfection of human knowledge. No more than Augustine did he look upon all truth as purely subjective; there was objective truth, to be sure, but, again in the manner of Augustine, he was never one to view this truth in isolation. And though he brought truth into relation with himself, he seldom evinced a personal practical interest in that truth. His tone was almost unreasonably dispassionate, as though it were immaterial to him whether a particular truth or body of truths had any consequences either for him or for anyone else.

Finally, as biographers and critics have repeatedly noted, he was patently not interested in formulating a rigid theological structure, in which all loose ends should be precisely accounted for, or, if that were impossible, should at least be noted as loose ends. He was content to write, never *ex professo*, of course, of what he knew and of what to him was unknowable and mysterious, and to let the loose ends simply lie where they chanced to fall.

But while Hawthorne himself was unsystematic in the presentation of his beliefs, it will be necessary to treat them in logical sequence. To that end, the first portion of this work will concern itself with his views on the existence and the attributes of God.

2

In his article, "Hawthorne and 'The Man of God,'"
Mr. Manning Hawthorne writes:

It may be that Chever [*sic*], like many of the "Orthodox,"
was offended because in none of Hawthorne's writings is
there any recognition of the Orthodox tenets of religion.
"His books might have been written by a Mahometan, so
far as any recognition of the great principles of Christianity
are concerned," was the remark of one who held fast the old
Orthodox faith according to John Calvin.[5]

Nathaniel Hawthorne, it is true, did not subscribe to
every clause of "the old Orthodox faith according to
John Calvin."   But his writings are replete with both
explicit and implicit confessions of a belief in the indispensable tenet of every "Orthodox" religion, namely, the
existence of God.

Throughout the notebooks, American, English, French
and Italian, there are numerous references to God, references which indicate the actual belief of the writer in the
existence of the traditionally accepted Supreme Being.

From *The American Notebooks,* this passage is representative:

     The above disappointment [a June frost], however, is
but a trifle to another, which, I fear, has befallen us within
a day or two.   Let my dearest wife record it, if she will; or
perhaps it may be better not to shadow another page with
such a recital.   God can restore all.   Let us trust that He
will (p. 185).

Clearly, this passage, written as it is in a journal not
meant for publication, demonstrates the personal belief
of its author in the traditional God.   Hawthorne is not
the man to append religious cliches to his paragraphs.
There is no question here of his giving mere lip-service
to an orthodox tenet in which he himself does not believe.

So, too, this typical passage from *The English Notebooks* is to be interpreted in the same light: "I thank God that I saw this Cathedral again, and thank Him that he inspired the builder to make it, and that mankind has so long enjoyed it" (p. 545).

A more specific profession of belief in the true God, coupled with an act of faith, occurs in *The French and Italian Notebooks*.

I looked again, and for a good while, at Carlo Dolce's portrait of the Eternal Father. . . . It is the All-powerless, a fair-haired, soft, consumptive Deity, with a mouth that has fallen open through very weakness; he holds one hand on his stomach, as if the wickedness and wretchedness of mankind made him qualmish; and he seems to be looking down out of heaven, with an expression of pitiable appeal, or as if seeking somewhere for assistance in his heavy task of ruling the Universe. . . . No wonder that wrong gets the better of right, and that good and ill are confounded, and everything gone higgledy-piggledy, if the Supreme Head were as here depicted; for I never saw—and nobody else ever saw—so perfect a representation of a person burthened with a task infinitely above his strength. If Carlo Dolce had been wicked enough to know what he was doing, the picture would have been most blasphemous—a satire, in the very person of the Almighty, against all incompetent rulers, and against the ricketty machine and crazy action of the Universe which He contrived. Heaven forgive me for such thoughts as this picture has suggested! [6]

Not only the notebooks, but the letters bear constant witness to Hawthorne's belief in God. Time after time, the complimentary close centers about the Deity. "God bless you and Your [*sic*] friend, Nath." (to Horatio Bridge, February 8, 1838); "God keep you from East winds and every other evil" (to Sophia Peabody, April 19, 1838); "God bless them [my mother and sisters], and us, and everybody. Dost thou perceive how love widens my heart?" (to Sophia Peabody, June 20, 1842). In letters to Sophia Peabody, dated November 25, 1839, and November 30, [1839], he signs himself "Deodatus" [given by God], the Latin equivalent of the Hebrew word *Nathaniel.*

As the letters and the notebooks, so, too, do the novels attest their author's belief in a Supreme Being. Lest citation become an end in itself, one passage of purely authorial comment, typical of many others, must suffice. "And while the other doves flew far and wide in quest of what was good for them, Hilda likewise spread her wings, and sought such ethereal and imaginative sustenance as God ordains for creatures of her kind" (*MF,* VI, 73).

3

One of the primary functions which the New England novelist attributes to the God in whose existence he firmly believes is that of creation. References to the Deity as Creator, in the strict sense of the term, occur frequently in all of his writings.

In a contribution to *The American Magazine of Useful and Entertaining Knowledge* (issue of March, 1836), of which he was at the time editor, Hawthorne hopes it will not be irrelevant to say "that the Creator gave us our world, in a certain sense, unfinished, and left it to the ingenuity of man to bring it to the highest perfection of which final [finite] and physical things are susceptible." [7] This passage, incidentally, cannot be interpreted as circumscribing the creative omnipotence of God. The parenthetical phrase *in a certain sense* precludes that possibility. For the rest, it may reasonably be assumed that Hawthorne is but transferring to the physical order an approach already well established in the spiritual order, namely, that man can and must cooperate in the salvation of his soul. An entry in *The French and Italian Notebooks* proves quite conclusively Hawthorne's conviction that God as Creator knows no limits: ". . . for certainly," he writes, "it was within God's power to create beings who should communicate with nature by innumerable other senses than these few which we possess." [8]

As to the objects created, Hawthorne is, of course, much less specific than the dramatic account in the initial chapters of the Book of Genesis. He refers to the world's "first formation by the Almighty"; [9] he thinks it one of "the mysteries of this present state, why monkies [*sic*] were made. The Creator," he feels certain, "could not surely have meant to ridicule his own work"; [10] he professes his belief that in the "small strain of [a bird's] music we recognize the voice of the Creator as distinctly as in the loudest accents of his thunder," [11] that "the flowers still sen[d] a fresh and sweet incense up to their Creator"; [12] he insists that God made even those "ugly people" with whom his wife was forced to sit for "an hour-and-a-half in that tobacco-smoky tavern"; [13] finally, as though by way of summation, he views the sunshine as typical of "the radiance of the Creator's face, expressing his love for all the creatures of his hand." [14]

Hawthorne, of course, encounters the usual doubts almost inseparable from a belief in the doctrine of creation. Not only does he find it strange that God should have created monkeys, as though ridiculing His own work. He also asks himself, at sight of a child in an English asylum, who had inherited "nothing but disease and vice" and who, as he puts it, would serve only "to vitiate and enervate" the human race, "Did God make this child? Has it a soul capable of immortality?—of immortal bliss? I am afraid not. At all events, it is quite beyond my conception and understanding." [15]

The denial, "I am afraid not," can, it is true, be logically interpreted as referring only to the latter question, in which case the creation of the child would not be impugned, even on the basis of this isolated passage. But granting that here Hawthorne seems to deny God's creation of a human being, it must also be granted that his final statement on the matter is one of submission to the doctrine: "God created this being, but I surely can't understand why he should have done so." In a quite similar passage he returns to the same problem: ". . . it puzzles me to think what they [the animals] were all made for; though, after all, it is quite as mysterious why man himself was made." [16] In neither case, however, does he deny God's creation of animals and human beings; he merely finds it sometimes hard to understand, on the purely natural level, why they should have been created. That *why*, therefore, is not a theological *why*. Hawthorne seems never to have posed the question which automatically presented itself to such Puritan divines as Jonathan Edwards: Why should a perfectly excellent Being create a world in which the majority of human beings will be damned forever?

Viewed in their totality, then, and particularly when gauged in conjunction with the occasional substitution of the word "Maker" for Creator,[17] Hawthorne's statements warrant the conclusion that the God in whom he believes is the God who created the earth and all things therein. No evidence exists to justify the speculation that he was an implicit evolutionist. With no less fervor than the grade-school pupil reciting his first catechism lesson, Hawthorne would have given the traditional answers to the questions: "Who made the world?" "Who made everything in the world?"

4

It has been established, thus far, that Hawthorne
recognizes the existence of God and attributes to this
God a primary causality. But that Supreme Deity of his
is far more than Creator, far more than the depersonal-
ized First Cause of the deists. He is a personal God, at
once Creator and Father of all mankind, maintaining an
unremitting supervision over and interest in His creatures.

In looking upon God as Someone who keeps His hand
in even the most minute affairs of His creatures, Hawthorne is at one with the theologians of Puritanism. It
was not sufficient for the Puritan theocrats to imagine
"that God organized a mechanical world and merely set
the first wheel in motion . . . God must be more than
the original designer of the creation, He must continu-
ously create it anew out of His infinite stores of being." [18]
The very roll of the dice and the sequence of the cards
were determined by God; and since divine providence
would thus be prostituted to unworthy ends, the Puritans
objected strenuously to these games. Now the God in
whom Hawthorne believes is this God of the Puritans;
unlike them, however, he did not stress the sovereignty
of God [19] to the almost total exclusion of every other of
His attributes save justice.

The traditional Puritans, in other words, believed in a
personal God. But they viewed this God as a Deity
interested in them only in so far as they were predestined
either for heaven or for hell. It was as though God Himself were watching every move they made, not with the
benign countenance of a Father, but with the eye of an
absolute Being striving to assure Himself that He had
rightfully damned the majority of them. Now it is precisely his insistence upon the fatherliness of God that
distinguishes the Hawthornian concept of God from that
of his Puritan ancestors. And, concomitantly too,

whereas the New England Calvinists taught that man's ultimate principle of conduct was his obligation to seek the salvation of his soul, Hawthorne, so far as can be judged, showed a decided inclination to abandon that principle and substitute for it man's happiness as the ultimate norm of conduct. "My business," he writes, "is merely to live and to enjoy; and whatever is essential to life and enjoyment will come as naturally as the dew from Heaven. This is—practically, at least—my faith." [20] Logically, therefore, Hawthorne's God was a humane, paternal, benignly providential God, interested in the earthly happiness of His children.

Reasonably too, then, Hawthorne could speak of Him in terms quite foreign to the Puritan mind.

In short, I have nothing to wish for—except, perhaps, that Providence would make it somewhat more plain to my apprehension how I am to earn my bread, after a year or two. [21]

Doubtless, God has planned how to make us happy; but thy husband, being of a distrustful and rebellious nature, cannot help wishing sometimes, that our Father would let him into His plans. [22]

I wonder, I wonder, I wonder, where on earth we are to set up our tabernacle. God knows;—but I want to know too. [23]

These excerpts indicate the filial and trustful attitude which Hawthorne maintained toward God as a Father interested in his temporal happiness. Frequent references throughout the novels and tales prove quite conclusively, if further proof be needed, that for this descendant of the Puritans the concept of God the Father, or Providence, was inextricably bound up with the concept of God the Creator. Hilda, in *The Marble Faun* (VI, 401), sobs out a prayer, "she hardly knew to whom, whether Michael, the Virgin, or the Father," a prayer that the burden of her spirit might be lightened a little. In *The House of the Seven Gables* (III, 225 f.), in a sentence of purely authorial comment, Hawthorne voices his opinion that, "in consequence of an unfortunate overdoing of a work praiseworthy in itself, the proceedings against the witches had proved far less acceptable to the Beneficent Father than to that very Arch Enemy whom they were intended to distress and utterly overwhelm." He describes Hester Prynne as entering a church, "trusting to share the Sabbath smile of the Universal Father" (V, 109).

Though stressing the attribute of providential paternality, Hawthorne, no more than the Puritans, minimized the inscrutability of God's counsels. Never one to engage in academic religious disputations, or even to take cognizance of them save perhaps in so far as to admit the impossibility of coming to a decision concerning them,[24] he made no attempt theologically to account for this inscrutability. New England's Puritan divines sought to explain the incomprehensibility of God's designs by distinguishing between His secret will and His revealed will. "His secret Will is His decree of what shall be, His revealed Will is His command of what ought to be."[25] This distinction never occurred to the author of *The Scarlet Letter*. For him, belief in God the Father and in His essential goodness was in no way contradictory to his acceptance of the Pauline exclamation: "How incomprehensible are His judgments, and how unsearchable His ways!" (Romans, 11: 33)

In his earliest full-length work, *Fanshawe,* Ellen is well aware that "there was none to help her, except that Being with whose inscrutable purposes it might consist to allow the wicked to triumph for a season, and the innocent to be brought low" (XI, 196). Commenting upon Clifford's strange plight, Hawthorne conjectures that perhaps he [Clifford] saw "in the mirror of his deeper consciousness, that he was an example and representative of that great class of people whom an inexplicable Providence is continually putting at cross-purposes with the world: breaking what seems its own promise in their nature; withholding their proper food, and setting poison before them for a banquet; and thus—when it might so easily, as one would think have been adjusted otherwise—making their existence a strangeness, a solitude, and torment" (*HSG,* III, 181).

In a very similar passage from his final major work, *The Marble Faun,* Hawthorne reflects upon Kenyon's attempt to find assurance that Hilda has come to no harm. "Providence," Kenyon consoles himself, "would keep a little area and atmosphere about her as safe and wholesome as heaven itself. . . ." Immediately thereafter, Hawthorne, clearly speaking now for himself, adds:

But these reflections were of slight avail. No doubt they were the religious truth. Yet the ways of Providence are utterly inscrutable; and many a murder has been done, and many an innocent virgin has lifted her white arms, beseeching its aid in her extremity, and all in vain; so that, though Providence is infinitely good and wise,—and perhaps for that very reason,—it may be half an eternity before the great circle of its scheme shall bring us the super-abundant recompense for all these sorrows! (VI, 470 f.)

Two conclusions concerning Hawthorne's belief in Providence are to be drawn from the passage just quoted:

1. God's ways are unintelligible to man;
2. God's ways are nevertheless "good and wise."

Should this twofold conclusion find acceptance, as it surely does on the part of Hawthorne, then it is only logical to assume that he would profess a childlike trust in the providence of God. Writing in *The American Magazine of Useful and Entertaining Knowledge,* issue of May, 1836, he admits that it is not at all hard to believe that Adam wept—"no marvel, if he [Adam] failed to discern, in this dreadful misery of his descendants, the

hand of a beneficent Creator." [26]   And there is more
than a touch of irony in his authorial remark that the
Italians are perhaps morally better off than the Ameri-
cans in so far as they seldom dream of being philanthropic; "they, at all events, cannot well pride themselves, as our own more energetic benevolence is apt to
do, upon sharing in the counsels of Providence and
kindly helping out its otherwise impracticable designs"
(*MF*, VI, 309).   Of importance in these two citations
is Hawthorne's statement, once again, that, despite all
appearances to the contrary, the Creator is unchange-
ably beneficent, that His designs are not impractical.
True, they do at times prove deceiving to the human
mind, as he expressly declares in a letter to Sophia Peabody, dated November 17, 1839:

Yet what could I say, but to assure you that I love you, and
partake whatever of good or evil God sends you—or rather,
partake whatever good God send you, whether it come in
festal garments or mourning ones; for still it is good, whether
arrayed in sable, or flower-crowned.

As has been noted, Hawthorne found it unnecessary,
perhaps even impossible, to enter into theological speculation concerning this inscrutability.   But he had arrived
at a personal understanding of the problem by the very
simple expedient of viewing a range of mountains from
a great distance and noting how both the lowest and the
loftiest of them are necessary to contribute to the "one
grand and beautiful idea." [27]   Seen from close at hand,
this aspect of grandeur remains unnoticed.   And so it is
with the designs of Almighty God.   Man can only, in
virtue of his finiteness, his partial scope of vision, see
each separate design in isolation; were it possible for him
to stand off at a distance, and see the total design, he
would be in admiration of the beauty and the reasonable-
ness of the whole structure.   It is this notion that Haw-

thorne has Kenyon express when, from the summit of Donatello's tower, he looks out upon the wide expanse of the Umbrian Valley:

"Thank God for letting me again behold this scene!" said the sculptor, a devout man in his way, reverently taking off his hat. "I have viewed it from many points, and never without as full a sensation of gratitude as my heart seems capable of feeling. How it strengthens the poor human spirit in its reliance on His providence, to ascend but this little way above the common level, and so attain a somewhat wider glimpse of His dealings with mankind! He doeth all things right! His will be done!" (*MF,* VI, 297 f.)

To the eye and mind of man, then, the counsels of Providence seem impractical, haphazard, even unjust. But that is only because man, being necessarily limited, cannot take the long-range view. He is in no position to get a general conspectus of the infinite designs of God. Lacking this, he has only his faith—Hawthorne would possibly call it his intuition, his inner feeling, which he valued above his understanding [28]—to guide him. Confronted by Carlo Dolce's portrait of "the All-powerless," he asks Heaven to forgive him "for such thoughts as this picture has suggested." [29] *The Three Fates* of Michelangelo, he records in his notebooks, "are a great work, containing and representing the very idea that makes a belief in Fate such a cold torture to the human soul. God give me a sure belief in his Providence." [30]

5

The occurrence of the terms *fate* and *Providence* in the passage just quoted brings into sharp focus one of the major problems in Hawthorne. How is one to reconcile, if reconciliation is possible, his acceptance of both fate and Providence? Commentators in the past either have chosen to bypass the difficulty or have stressed the element of fate. In the latter case, Hawthorne emerges as a believer in absolute determinism.

It would be folly to deny that there is here a definite problem. But a close study of the numerous passages in which Hawthorne uses the words *fate, destiny, evil destiny, doom* seems to indicate that the New Englander is guilty of nothing more than failure to heed the Augustinian admonition, "If anyone gives the name of fate to God's will or power, let him keep his opinion, but mend his speech." [31]

For Boethius, in his *Consolations of Philosophy,* defines fate as "a disposition inherent in changeable things, by which providence connects each one with its proper order." [32] Not only does this definition show that fate can coexist with providence, but it provides a basis whereby fate and providence can be logically differentiated. That basis is clearly the phrase *inherent in changeable things.* In other words, *providence* is the term used to refer to the order as existing in the mind of God and not yet impressed on things; *fate* is the term used to refer to this same order as already expressed in things. The adjective *changeable,* to complete the analysis, indicates that providence does not deprive things of contingency or changeableness. [33]

With this distinction in mind, one can now examine one or the other of Hawthorne's typical statements. "As the animosity of fate would have it, there was a great influx of custom in the course of the afternoon" (*HSG,* III, 88). It is to be noted that the event has already occurred: "there was a great influx of custom in the course of the afternoon." Hawthorne, therefore, is properly speaking of an order "already expressed in things," and, in accordance with the Boethian distinction, is using the term quite legitimately. Nor does the attribution of animosity to this fate render the previous argument invalid, for to the finite mind of man, as Hawthorne well knew, the designs and the workings out of Providence may indeed seem unjust. "Life," he wrote, "is made up of marble and mud. And, without all the deeper trust in a comprehensive sympathy above us, we might hence be led to suspect the insult of a sneer, as well as an immitigable frown, on the iron countenance of fate" (*HSG*, III, 59). In this passage, once again, the term *fate* is used in the Boethian sense, expressing an order or a result already accomplished, which, without a belief in "a comprehensive sympathy," in Providence, would seem unreasonable and unkind.

Commenting upon the attempts of the man who would build up vast estates in order that the next generation might inherit them, Hawthorne writes, "He lays his own dead corpse beneath the underpinning, as one may say, and hangs his frowning picture on the wall, and, after thus converting himself into an evil destiny, expects his remotest great-grandchildren to be happy there" (*HSG*, III, 312). In this sentence, the words *evil destiny* are evidently synonymous with the term *fate*. Again, the reference is clearly to an already accomplished fact: the conversion "into an evil destiny" has already occurred. The Boethian distinction is therefore applicable, as it is to three other passages in which the term *destiny* is used of Judge Pyncheon or of his ilk.[34] In "The Artist of the Beautiful," Hawthorne states that the marriage of Annie to Danforth "was the very perversity of fate that makes human existence appear too absurd and contradictory to be the scene of one other hope or one other fear" (II, 523). Once again, the marriage has already taken place: a complex series of causes has effected the present situation. The result appears—but only *appears*—to be absurd and contradictory.

A similar analysis is surely possible of Zenobia's words to Priscilla: "You have been my evil fate . . ." (*BR*, V,

569). And referring to Hester's seeming inability, in the forest scene, to rid herself of the scarlet letter, Hawthorne notes: "So it ever is, whether thus typified or not, that an evil deed invests itself with the character of doom" (V, 253). But here again the term *doom*—or *fate* or *destiny,* words which might just as easily have been substituted—may mean nothing more than that sometimes highly complex "concatenation of causes acting under the will of God, by which any given event is influenced." [35] Such a concatenation of causes, in which, for example, each succeeding event or sin seems to flow almost necessarily from its predecessor—much in the same way as one lie begets another, until the prevaricator finds himself hopelessly enmeshed in untruth—may, in its final stages, bring with it a serious diminution of free will. Yet the fact remains that, at every stage, the sinner retains sufficient freedom to retrace his steps, to right the wrong, or at least to repent of it. Strictly speaking, as will become clear in the chapter on the "unpardonable" sin, there is for the New England novelist no such spiritual condition as "a point of no return." However, if the sinner does not recant, Hawthorne would then speak of his first lapse from righteousness as a "deed invest [ing] itself with the character of doom." But that this phrase is not to be construed as an implicit profession of belief in the doctrine of absolute determinism is clear, not only from Hawthorne's constant reference to man's freedom of will,[36] but even from such chance statements as the one in which Hollingsworth held before his pupils "the possibility of a worthier life than that which had become their fate" (*BR,* V, 469).

The routine compilation of pertinent passages on the subject under discussion indicates that the terms *fate, destiny,* and *doom* occur far more often in the fictional than in the non-fictional writings of Hawthorne.[37] No particular significance, however, need be attached to this phenomenon, since it can readily be accounted for by the fact that the terms in question are generally associated with untoward events, happenings which bring sorrow and distress to the parties involved and which for that very reason seem to place God's providence in an unfavorable light: the terms, as used by Hawthorne, do connote a certain animosity. Now with this pattern of usage once established, it is only natural that the artificially manipulated sequences of the novels and tales should provide a more abundant opportunity for words betokening a seeming animosity than the journals and letters.

When Hawthorne, then, in the passage which provided the springboard for this necessary digression, prays that God may give him "a sure belief in his Providence," as opposed to the cold torture of a belief in fate, he is using the terms in a mutually exclusive sense. This is clear from Mrs. Hawthorne's comments on her husband's reaction to *The Three Fates* of Michelangelo: "The weird sister who stands in the middle seemed to me to have a slight compunction in her mouth and eyes, but Mr. Hawthorne said she had not to him, and that 'if she had, she would not be a Fate, but a Providence.' " [38] Fate there means for him a mechanically contrived and heartless arrangement of events precluding the free operation of the will both of God and of man. But Hawthorne does not believe in such a fatalistic arrangement, as is evident from this very passage, from the whole context of his thought concerning the attributes of the Supreme Being, and from the close examination of typical questionable passages.

If Hawthorne's belief in a Deity who is at once the Creator and the Paternal Governor of the universe be viewed in isolation, he may justifiably be classified either as a Puritan or as a Unitarian. He diverges sharply from the true Puritan outlook, however, in his insistence upon the mercy of Almighty God, an attribute which New England Calvinism had buried beneath the weight of His awful and arbitrary sovereignty.

A brief conspectus of the Calvinistic and Arminian (or pre-Unitarian) teaching on this point will serve to render more definite Hawthorne's theological position.

The Reverend Charles Chauncy of Boston proposed, in opposition to the accepted teaching, that the First Cause, who is by definition wise and powerful and good, "shall prevail upon all men, and prepare them, in a moral way, as moral agents, for an eternal reign in happy life." [39] Many men, according to Chauncy, will go to hell, but they will not stay there; they will be there only long enough to be purified and thus to become worthy of heaven. God, in other words, is moved by benevolence to man, not by a desire to show forth His justice. And since, in the view of the Universalists, the end of God in creation was the happiness of His creatures, they insisted upon such attributes as goodness and wisdom, power and mercy. Justice and arbitrary sovereignty were quite unnecessary.

This Universalism of Chauncy was attacked by Samuel Hopkins [40] and Joseph Bellamy,[41] among others, who insisted, in their best Calvinistic dialectic, that the "wrath of God in relation to sin is an integral part of His glory for the display of which . . . He created the world. . . . If the misery of the sinner is conducive to such a display, which it must be because sinners are in fact miserable, then it is just and good that sinners should be punished with misery." [42]

The radical shift from Calvinism is perhaps best and most succinctly pointed up by saying that Chauncy and his associates had identified the glory of God with the happiness of His creatures. "Before, the good of man consisted ultimately in glorifying God; now [with Chauncy], the glory of God consists in the good of man." [43]

With this doctrinally important divergence in mind, it is now possible to gauge more accurately Hawthorne's position.

As already mentioned, Hawthorne states quite clearly: "My business is merely to live and to enjoy; and whatever is essential to life and enjoyment will come as naturally as the dew from Heaven. This is—practically, at least—my faith." [44] Accepting this profession of faith at its face value, it is clear that Hawthorne has aligned himself with the Arminians as opposed to the traditional New England Calvinists. The happiness of man is of primary concern; he makes no mention of the glory of God.

It is not strange, accordingly, that his writings should contain frequent references to God's love and care for His creatures. Prior to narrating the episode in which Clifford and Hepzibah try to attend Sunday services, he writes by way of preface: "In the incident now to be sketched, there was a touching recognition, on Clifford's part, of God's care and love towards him,—towards the poor, forsaken man, who, if any mortal could, might have been pardoned for regarding himself as thrown aside, forgotten, and left to be the sport of some fiend, whose playfulness was an ecstasy of mischief" (*HSG*, III, 201). The words *care and love* are, of course, in Clifford's thought trend, but the explicit elucidation after the dash [—], including the significant unreal clause, *if any mortal could,* is Hawthorne speaking authorially. Later in the same novel he pauses to reprimand Hepzibah for her failure to understand that, "just as there comes a warm sunbeam into every cottage window, so comes a lovebeam of God's care and pity for every separate need" (III, 291).

A notable passage from *The Blithedale Romance* is particularly pertinent to the present demonstration. Zenobia had committed suicide; her body had been recovered from the waters; and she was exposed to the gaze of the spectators. Had she been saved, even though her final action was a violation of God's canon against self-slaughter? Coverdale, the *I* of the tale, voices a belief that is a virtual profession of faith in God's infinite mercy.

The flitting moment after Zenobia sank into the dark pool—when her breath was gone, and her soul at her lips—was as long, in its capacity of God's infinite forgiveness, as the lifetime of the world! (V, 586)

Likewise, Hawthorne objects to Michelangelo's *Last Judgment* because it presents the Saviour as an "inexorable Judge"; it seems to him "very undesirable that he should ever be represented in that aspect, when it is so essential to our religion to believe him infinitely kinder and better towards us than we deserve." [45] But he approves of Fra Angelico, because in his fresco he portrays "Jesus, with the throng of blessed saints around him, and a flow of tender and powerful love in his own face, that ought to suffice to redeem all the damned, and convert the very fiends, and quench the fires of hell by its holier light." Fra Angelico, he adds, had "a higher conception of his Saviour than Michael Angelo did." [46]

Further references to the divine mercy as an attribute specifically proper to the Son of God will appear in the succeeding portion of this chapter. [47] But enough evi-

dence has been submitted to show clearly that Hawthorne subordinates the glory of God to the happiness of
man, that, practically speaking, his position is homo-
centric rather than theocentric. Since, however, his
belief in the existence and nature of God is unshakable,
he compromises, as it were, and stresses God's care and
goodness and mercy rather than His sovereignty and
glory. This, of course, distinguishes him sharply from
the New England proponents of Calvinism—Edwards,
Bellamy, Hopkins—and puts him well on the road to
Arminianism.

7

The doctrinal paths of most early-nineteenth-century
New Englanders led from Puritanism through Arminianism to Unitarianism. Since Hawthorne had clearly set
his foot along Arminian ways, it seemed legitimate to
assume that he would embrace Unitarianism. F. P.
Stearns, in fact, implies that such was indeed the case:
"It is presumable that Nathaniel Hawthorne also became
a Unitarian, so far as he can be considered a sectarian
at all . . ." [48] And George Willis Cooke, in his *Unitarianism in America,* remarks that no man "who has
written in this country . . . was more deeply influenced
than he [Hawthorne] by those spiritual ideas and traditions which may be properly called Unitarian." [49]

But it is patently impossible to classify Hawthorne as a
Unitarian, even an implicit one. For in the belief of the
Unitarians, Christ was no more than a human being who
led his fellowmen to a greater knowledge of God. Concomitantly, they rejected the Virgin Birth, the redemption, and the resurrection of the Saviour.

Now it cannot be demonstrated that Hawthorne maintained a traditional Trinitarianism against the encroaches
of Unitarianism: I find no adequate proof of a belief in

the Holy Spirit, the third person of the Trinity. But his belief in a Redeemer, in a Son of God who partakes of the same nature as the Father, is readily demonstrable.

That Hawthorne considers Christ as equal God with the Father appears from his reactions to various Italian works of art. The nature of his comments on these occasions indicates that he finds in such paintings a reflection of his own beliefs. He is not, in other words, accommodating himself to the religious tenets of the artist for the sole purpose of inducing a state of aesthetic appreciation.

As for his [an Englishman touring the Uffizi Gallery] criticisms, I am sorry to remember only one; it was upon the picture of the nativity, by Correggio, in the Tribune, where the mother is kneeling before the child, and adoring it in an awful rapture, because she sees the Eternal God in its baby-face and figure.[50]

And sometimes, amid these sensual images, I caught the divine pensiveness of a Madonna's face, or the glory and majesty of the babe Jesus in her lap, with his Father shining through him. This is a sort of revelation, whenever it comes.[51]

But in this picture the Virgin had a look as if she were loving the infant as her own flesh and blood, and at the same time giving him an awful worship as to her Creator.[52]

These three excerpts, while naturally not as conclusive as an Athanasian creed, seem to affirm their author's belief in a Child, called Jesus, born of a woman, at once God ["her Creator"; "she sees the Eternal God in its baby-face and figure"] and man ["the Virgin had a look as if she were loving the infant as her own flesh and blood"]. Admittedly, it is possible, on the basis of the quotations adduced, to challenge the deduction that Hawthorne believes in the twofold nature of Christ, the divine and the human. His divinity, however, is definitely mentioned in other passages.   The author-observer in *The Blithedale Romance* notes that every masculine theologist has been prone to mingle an intellectual alloy with deep religious sentiment—"save only One, who merely veiled himself in mortal and masculine shape, but was, in truth, divine" (V, 458).   Referring to Sodoma's fresco of Christ bound to the pillar, he writes: "Even in this extremity, however, he is still divine . . . He is as much, and as visibly, our Redeemer, there bound, there fainting, and bleeding from the scourge, with the cross in view, as if he sat on his throne of glory in the heavens" (*MF*, VI, 387).[53]

This Christ was born on Christmas Day—the "holiest of holydays—the day that brought ransom to all other sinners" [save "us miserable Custom-House officers," who have to work tomorrow].[54]

This Christ suffered for men.

Occasionally, today, I was sensible of a certain degree of emotion in looking at an old picture; as for example, by a large, dark, ugly picture of Christ bearing the cross and sinking beneath it, when, somehow or other, a sense of his agony, and the fearful wrong that mankind did to its Redeemer, and the scorn of his enemies and sorrow of those that loved him, came knocking at my heart, and partly got entrance there.[55]

Christ died for men, and rose to glory.

These impure pictures [of nude Venuses] are from the same illustrious and impious hands that adventured to call before us the august forms of Apostles and Saints, the Blessed Mother of the Redeemer, and her Son, at his death, and in his glory, and even the awfulness of Him, to whom the martyrs, dead a thousand years ago, have not yet dared to raise their eyes.   They seem to take up one task or the other—the disrobed woman . . . or the type of highest and tenderest womanhood in the mother of their Saviour—with equal readiness . . . (*MF*, VI, 384).

Traditionally and properly associated with the God who redeemed mankind are the attributes of love and mercy. These, too, Hawthorne ascribes to the Second Person of the Trinity.

Thus, while the fertile scene showed the never-failing bene-ficence of the Creator towards man in his transitory state, these symbols [crown of thorns, spear, sponge] reminded each wayfarer of the Saviour's infinitely greater love for him as an immortal spirit (*MF,* VI, 341).

A very relevant entry in *The French and Italian Note-books* records Hawthorne's impressions of *The Last Judgment,* as well as his belief in the goodness of God.

. . . above sits Jesus, not looking in the least like the Savior of the world, but with uplifted arm denouncing eter-nal misery on those whom he came to save. I fear I am myself among the wicked, for I found myself inevitably tak-ing their part, and asking for at least a little pity, some few regrets, and not such a stern denunciatory spirit on the part of Him who had thought us worth dying for. . . . It would be a very terrible picture to one who should really see Jesus, the Savior, in that inexorable Judge, but it seems to me very undesirable that he should ever be represented in that aspect, when it is so essential to our religion to believe him infinitely kinder and better towards us than we deserve.[56]

While Hawthorne's tendency to stress the kindness and mercy of the Saviour shows once again his Arminianism, this passage does prove his belief in a Christ who came to save mankind by His death. Naturally, no one ex-cerpt, nor any combination of excerpts, for that matter, proves Hawthorne's unqualified acceptance of the full doctrine of a redeeming God-Man. The passages already quoted, however, if taken as a unit, justify the statement that Hawthorne did believe in Christ and attributed to Him the work of redemption.

It is likewise impossible to find in Hawthorne any

declaration which would definitely prove his belief in the doctrine of the Virgin Birth, though there are indications that he attributed to Mary a superior place in the scheme of the redemption.   Nowhere does he specifically allude to Christ's having been "conceived by the Holy Ghost." He does, however, refer to Mary authorially as "the Virgin mother" (*MF*, VI, 342); Hilda, speaking as Hilda, maintains that a Christian girl—"even a daughter of the Puritans—may surely pay honor to the idea of divine Womanhood, without giving up the faith of her forefathers" (VI, 71); and the narrator of *The Blithedale Romance* admits that he has "always envied the Catholics their faith in that sweet, sacred Virgin Mother, who stands between them and the Deity, intercepting somewhat of his awful splendor, but permitting his love to stream upon the worshipper more intelligibly to human comprehension through the medium of a woman's tenderness" (V, 458).   In this last instance Hawthorne expresses very well the traditional doctrine of Mary as the mediatrix of all grace.

It may be suggested at this point that Hawthorne's frequent mention of the Virgin Mother in *The French and Italian Notebooks* as well as the numerous references to her in *The Marble Faun* may be partially accounted for by the historical events of the decade in which he was writing.   In 1858, the Blessed Virgin appeared to Bernadette Soubirous at Lourdes, France. Detailed reports of this manifestation, as well as of the miracles following it, were widely disseminated in Rome. And the declaration of Mary, "I am the Immaculate Conception," by which she made known to Bernadette her identity, created all the more interest in the light of the official dogmatic definition of the Immaculate Conception four years previously.   But while these significant events in the history of Catholicism may have heightened his appreciation of God's mother, it would be wrong to maintain that her place in *The Marble Faun* is merely an instance of the author's accommodating himself to his historical setting. The Blessed Virgin is too closely interwoven with Hilda's life to be nothing more than an historical afterthought. Even if this were the case, however, it would not account for the numerous Marian passages in *The French and Italian Notebooks,* nor for the classic expression, already quoted, of Mary's mediatrixship in *The Blithedale Romance.*

8

Any attempt to derive a definite pattern of belief from a body of writing as various as Hawthorne's is certain to be impeded by the discovery of isolated passages which seem to contradict the general trend of evidence. One such passage is an entry in *The English Notebooks,* under date of February 8, 1856. On that day Hawthorne read

St. Luke's account of the agony, the trial, the crucifixion, and the resurrection; and how Christ appeared to the two disciples on their way to Emmaus, and afterwards to a company of disciples. On both these latter occasions, he expounded the Scriptures to them, and showed the application of the old prophecies to himself; and it is to be supposed that he made them fully (or at least sufficiently) aware what his character was, whether God, or Man, or both, or something between;—together with all other essential points of doctrine. But none of this doctrine, or of these expositions, are recorded; the mere facts being most simply stated, and the conclusion to which he led them, that (whether God himself, or the Son of God, or merely the son of Man) he was, at all events, the Christ foretold in the Jewish Scriptures. This last, therefore, must have been the one essential point (p. 272).

It is to no avail to point out that Hawthorne ignores the context of the discussions entered into by the Lord and His disciples on those two occasions. Nor will it dissipate the difficulty seemingly inherent in the passage to note that "the Christ foretold in the Jewish Scriptures" was unmistakably represented there as divine, and that Hawthorne freely admitted "the prophetic truth of the Bible. It is not too much to say," he writes, "that all the countries, where the old prophets dwelt, are now strewn with accomplished prophecies."[57] For despite such observations as these, the difficulty remains: Hawthorne here seems to argue that it is really of minor importance whether Christ is God, or the Son of God, or the Son of Man, or something else. What is important is that He is the Christ foretold in the Old Testament.

Against those who would use this passage as controverting the arguments already presented, it may be pointed out that this excerpt of itself is valueless. It does not prove that Hawthorne believed Christ to be mere man. Nor does it show that he refused to make up his mind on the matter. All that can logically be deduced is that Hawthorne says this portion of St. Luke's Gospel proves nothing more than that the Christ of St. Luke is the Christ foretold in the Jewish Scriptures. Whether Hawthorne believed this Christ to be divine or not must still be determined, if it is to be determined at all, from other pertinent passages in his writings.

Likewise, there is no evidence to show that Hawthorne was inclined toward Manicheism, a belief which posits two omnipotent operating forces, one good, the other evil. Quite apart from the fact that such a view is a contradiction in itself, it is clear that the role Hawthorne assigns to the devil is thoroughly in accord with centuries-old Christian tradition. Satan is our Arch Enemy (*HSG*, III, 226); he sets snares for God's creatures (*SL*, V, 144) in order to tempt them to commit sin (*SL*, V, 103).[58] But he does all this subject to the divine permission (*SL*, V, 156). The devil is at odds with God and with man, but God alone is supreme and omnipotent. How it can be consonant with a kind and good God to permit the devil such a large sphere of operation is a difficulty of which Hawthorne takes no specific cognizance, though he may well have recurred to his oft expressed belief that the finite mind of man is not in a position of sufficient eminence to understand the incomprehensible designs of God.

9

A succeeding chapter of this work will deal exclusively with Hawthorne's opinions on various forms of institutionalized religion. Here it is enough to mention that his violent objections to Catholicism were almost entirely based on the contention that the morals of clerical and lay Catholics belie their ancient beliefs. Errant Catholic moral rather than errant Catholic dogma was at the bottom of his dissatisfaction with the Roman Catholic Church. It is therefore not surprising to find that the dogmas which he does accept are in substantial agreement with the parallel portion of a third-century Christian expression of faith called the Apostles' creed. The phrases enclosed in brackets find no explicit counterpart in Hawthorne.

I believe in God, the Father Almighty, Creator of Heaven and Earth, and in Jesus Christ, His only Son, Our Lord, Who was [conceived by the Holy Ghost,] born of the Virgin Mary, suffered [under Pontius Pilate], was crucified, died, and [was buried. The third day] He arose again from the dead, sitteth at the right hand of God the Father Almighty, from thence He shall come to judge the living and the dead.

NOTES

1 Herbert Wallace Schneider, *The Puritan Mind* (New York: Henry Holt and Company, 1930), p. 241.

2 Cf. Perry Miller, *The New England Mind* (New York: The Macmillan Company, 1939), p. 22: "The similarity of mood between Augustine and the Puritans could be illustrated merely by the frequency with which he is quoted in Puritan writing. . . . The high estimation in which Puritans held the name of Augustine is revealed

when Hooker continues to call him 'Saint,' though this use of the word was generally proscribed as a Popish corruption." That Hawthorne early made the acquaintance of St. Augustine is clear from an entry in his notebooks under date of September 7, 1835—cf. *Passages from the American Note-Books*, IX, 20. This conclusion finds probable corroboration in Julian Hawthorne's comment "he [Nathaniel Hawthorne] had read 'The Fathers of the Early Christian Church' "—cf. *The Memoirs of Julian Hawthorne* (New York: The Macmillan Company, 1938), p. 16.

3 Karl Adam, *Saint Augustine* (New York: The Macmillan Company, 1932), p. 6. The contrast between Augustine and Thomas Aquinas is developed in detail in this work of the great German theologian.

4 St. Augustine, *Epistola CXXX*, 15.

5 Manning Hawthorne, "Hawthorne and 'The Man of God,' " *The Colophon*, II (n.s.), 275.

6 *The French and Italian Notebooks*, III, 460.

7 Quoted in Arlin Turner, *Hawthorne as Editor* (University, Louisiana: Louisiana State University Press, 1941), p. 168.

8 *The French and Italian Notebooks*, III, 469.

9 *Ibid.*, II, 253.

10 *The English Notebooks*, p. 209.

11 *HSG*, III, 168.

12 *Ibid.*, III, 93.

13 *The American Notebooks*, p. 177.

14 "Egotism," II, 307.

15 *The English Notebooks*, p. 276.

16 *Ibid.*, p. 610.

17 *E.g., The French and Italian Notebooks*, II, 295.

18 Miller, *op. cit.*, p. 14. Cf. also Schneider, *op. cit.*, p. 48: "No event was merely natural; it was an act of God and was hence surcharged with that 'numinous' quality which gives birth to both prophetic insight and mystic illumination."

19 R. N. Carew Hunt, *Calvin* (London: The Century Press, 1933), pp. 114-140. In this portion of his work, entitled "Calvin's Theology and Ethics," Hunt views the insistence upon God's absolute sovereignty as the central principle of Calvin's theology.

20 *The American Notebooks*, p. 154.

21 Letter to Evert A. Duyckinck, November 26, 1843.

22 Letter to Sophia Peabody, April 19, 1840.

23 Letter to Sophia Peabody, February 27, 1842.

24 As previously indicated, this admission is implicit in Hawthorne's use of the devices of multiple choice and alternate possibilities.

25 Miller, *op. cit.*, p. 21.

26 Quoted in Turner, *op. cit.*, p. 176.

27 *The French and Italian Notebooks*, III, 712. The idea that all divergencies disappear when they are viewed from a commanding height is frequently stated throughout Hawthorne's works. Cf., for example, *The American Notebooks*, pp. 42, 119.

[28] Trying to evaluate his strange reaction to the various tales of spiritistic manifestations to which he listened, Hawthorne wrote: "They are facts to my understanding (which, it might have been anticipated, would have been the last to acknowledge them,) but they seem not to be facts to my intuitions and deeper perceptions. My inner soul does not in the least admit them. There is a mistake somewhere" (*The French and Italian Notebooks,* III, 495).

[29] *Ibid.,* III, 460.

[30] *Ibid.,* II, 374 f.

[31] St. Augustine, *De Civitate Dei,* V, i.

[32] Boethius, *De Consolatione,* IV.

[33] St. Thomas Aquinas, *Summa contra Gentiles,* III, xciii.

[34] *HSG,* III, 287, 293, 373.

[35] Vernon J. Bourke, *Augustine's Quest of Wisdom* (Milwaukee: The Bruce Publishing Company, 1945), p. 256.

[36] Cf. chapter II, section 9.

[37] For examples of the use of these terms in his non-fictional writings, cf. *The English Notebooks,* pp. 490, 491, 606; *The French and Italian Notebooks,* II, 51.

[38] Mrs. Nathaniel Hawthorne, *Notes in England and Italy* (New York, 1875), p. 369.

[39] Charles Chauncy, *The Mystery Hid from Ages and Generations* (London, 1784), p. 168.

[40] Hopkins propounds his views to best advantage in *The Future State of Those Who Die in Their Sins.*

[41] Bellamy asserts his position in an essay entitled *The Nature and Glory of the Gospel of Jesus Christ.*

[42] Joseph Haroutunian, *Piety Versus Moralism* (New York: Henry Holt and Company, 1932), pp. 142, 144.

[43] *Ibid.,* p. 145.

[44] *The American Notebooks,* p. 154.

[45] *The French and Italian Notebooks,* II, 255.

[46] *Ibid.,* II, 398.

[47] Cf. section 7.

[48] F. P. Stearns, *The Life and Genius of Nathaniel Hawthorne* (Philadelphia: J. B. Lippincott Company, 1906), p. 421.

[49] George Willis Cooke, *Unitarianism in America* (1902), p. 430.

[50] *The French and Italian Notebooks,* III, 528.

[51] *Ibid.,* II, 390.

[52] *The English Notebooks,* p. 555.

[53] Cf. also *The French and Italian Notebooks,* III, 564.

[54] Letter to Sophia Peabody, December 24, 1839.

[55] *The French and Italian Notebooks,* II, 358.

[56] *Ibid.,* II, 254 f.

[57] *The American Magazine of Useful and Entertaining Knowledge* (May, 1836), as quoted in Turner, *op. cit.,* p. 125.

[58] Cf. also *The American Notebooks,* p. 214.

Nevertheless, if we look through all the heroic fortunes of mankind, we shall find this same entanglement of something mean and trivial with whatever is noblest in joy and sorrow. Life is made up of marble and mud. And, without all the deeper trust in a comprehensive sympathy above us, we might hence be led to suspect the insult of a sneer, as well as an immitigable frown, on the iron countenance of fate.

—*The House of the Seven Gables,* III, 59.

II *Man*

In the post-Renaissance era, there have been two main bodies of thought concerning man, one of them centering itself around the Natural Man, the other, around the Frustrated Man. A brief examination of each will serve the double purpose of placing Hawthorne into the correct historical perspective and of clarifying to some extent the implications of his thinking concerning man.

The post-Renaissance concept of the Natural [Humanistic] Man derives ultimately, though quite accidentally, from Luther and the Protestant Reformation. According to the teaching of Luther, sin has vitiated man's nature in its very essence. This evil is final. Grace and the sacraments cover over, but do not wash away, original sin. As a culminating reaction against this doctrine of man's intrinsic depravity, Jean-Jacques Rousseau, 230 years after Luther, gave final, though somewhat ambiguous formulation to the concept of primitive Natural Goodness.

This concept, practically speaking, bases itself on the supposition that man "originally lived in a *purely natural* paradise of happiness and goodness, and that Nature herself will in future perform the function which grace fulfilled in the Catholic conception. It also means that such a state of happiness and goodness . . . is *natural* to man, that is to say, essentially required by our nature. Not only, then, is there no original sin of which we bear the guilt at our birth and still keep the wounds, not only is there in us no seat of concupiscence and unhealthy proclivities to incline us to evil, but, further, the state of suffering and hardship is one essentially *opposed to nature* . . . and our nature demands that we should, at any cost, be freed from it." [1]

Jacques Maritain admits that, in a very general way, the Rousseauist idea of Natural Goodness depends on the great current of naturalism flowing from the Renaissance and the Cartesian Reformation; its true origins, however, are to be sought "not only in the theory of the *good savage* invented by the imprudent apologetic of the missionaries of the eighteenth century, but also and much more thoroughly on one side, in the naturalization of the very idea of grace which we see develop in the school of Fenelon, on another side . . . in that heretical exaggeration of pessimism which so many historians go on taking for the Christian spirit, and which caused the privileges of the state of innocence to be regarded as due to human nature before it was *essentially corrupted* by original sin." [2]

Alongside this hypothesis, which derives from the premise that man can be explained without any reference to causes or influences outside of this universe, there developed the concept of the Frustrated Man. In sharp contrast to the naturally good and progressive man, the Frustrated Man is a "fallen man."

The Frustrated Man is one who has within himself some radical tension or dialectic—who is groaning for some kind of sublimation or deliverance. The Frustrated Man is the Old Testament without the New, the Fall without the Redemption, the tragedy of man without the hope of a Calvary. From a theological point of view, the concept represents the rediscovery of the doctrine of Original Sin . . . [3]

Prophetic of this Frustrated Man were Dostoevski and, paradoxically enough, Nietzsche. Dostoevski counter-

balanced the optimistic humanism of the last century by
stressing the inner struggle in man between the forces
of good and evil. For him the soul of man became a
battlefield, on which the struggle to sink to the depths
or to rise to the heights was in continuous progress.
Nietzsche, too, rejected the Natural Man; contrary to
Dostoevski, however, he viewed man, "not so much as
possessing a conflict within himself, but as being a unit
in the universal conflict between Christ and anti-Christ." [4]

The doctrine of the Frustrated Man has found its
adherents down to the present day: Soren Kierkegaard,
for whom man is a source of conflict and tension; Karl
Barth, with his *Theology of Crisis;* Reinhold Niebuhr,
who perhaps sums up best the conflict in man resulting
from his duality: "The obvious fact is that man is a child
of nature, subject to its vicissitudes, compelled by its
necessities, driven by its impulses. . . . The other less
obvious fact is that man is a spirit who stands outside of
nature, life, himself, his reason, and the world." [5]

The foregoing delineations of these two principal
post-Renaissance views concerning man are, necessarily,
somewhat oversimplified. But the main outlines are
clearly enough sketched to bring out the true nature of
each view. And it is equally clear to even the casual
student of Hawthorne's thought that the New England
novelist belongs to the Frustrated-Man school rather
than to the Natural-Man school. To an extraordinary
degree, Hawthorne was conscious of a duality in man—
a battle between spirit and matter, between man's potentialities and his realizations. That puts him squarely
in the camp of Dostoevski and Melville and Barth and
Niebuhr; that, too, distinguishes him sharply from Rousseau and Hegel and Emerson.

"One thing," writes Professor Norman Holmes Pearson, "will never be known of Hawthorne's years at Bowdoin. The *Sturm und Drang* of his emotional life remains an empty page. No evidence exists of any of those religious doubts and philosophical questionings which seem so essential a part of adolescence. He must have felt them, but his reticence kept them from the world. . . . We know the shell of his Bowdoin life; at the rest we can only guess."[6]

What is quite true of Hawthorne's college years is not true of his subsequent life. The record of his *Sturm und Drang* is preserved in his letters and journals, and, by ready inference, in his tales and romances. And while its manifestations are various, they invariably connote a basic dichotomy which sets up a very definite tension or conflict within him.

This personal conflict in the man, as has been said, shows itself in various ways. One such way has already been indicated: he found it difficult to decide whether to rely more upon his intuitions and deeper perceptions than upon his understanding.[7] That problem appeared in full force when he attempted to evaluate his strange reaction to the stories of spiritistic phenomena which he heard. His understanding, he noted, admitted these accounts as facts, but not his inner soul. In the passage in question he came to no definite conclusion, but his entire attitude toward such manifestations, on this and numerous other occasions, seems to indicate that in matters spiritistic he chose to attribute a greater validity to his intuitions than to his understanding.

The sight of stained glass windows led him to restate the same problem in another form. Light from heaven was necessary to make such windows visible. "If the church were merely illuminated from the inside—that is, by what light a man can get from his own understanding—the pictures would be invisible, or wear at best but a miserable aspect." [8] Such light from heaven shines through a man's inner perceptions, his intuitions.

Fundamentally, of course, the difficulty centering about the relative validity of intuition vs. understanding is but part of the larger problem of heart vs. head, "the conflict between conscientiousness and practical achievement, the conflict between Puritan and Yankee" [9]—the conflict, one may add, between idealism on the one hand and realism on the other. And the fact that his final verdict on the matter took the form of a decision against the validity of man's intuition is, at the moment, secondary; what is important is that Hawthorne experienced the conflicts and tensions incidental upon arriving at any decision at all.

A second aspect of the dichotomy in Hawthorne himself arises from his tendency to remain aloof from the ordinary acquaintanceships of life, while at the same time retaining his firm conviction that he dare not remain apart from the world in which he lived. While this isolationism of his has at times been grossly exaggerated, it is nevertheless true that he saw himself confronted with the problem of building "a distinct ethical self without turning all his faculties inward and becoming a mere worshipper of his own ego"; however, in avoiding this possibility, he could not afford to open "himself to the vital influences which could come to him only through his relations with other persons and with nature" to such an extent that he would run the risk of "relinquishing so much of his precious individuality . . . [as to] become a human cipher." [10]

As Pearson points out, Hawthorne's aloofness need not be interpreted as "a dislike of normal relationships so much as an inability to share in them." [11] Yet this extenuation by no means eliminates the possibility of tension; rather it enhances it all the more, particularly if it be remembered that Hawthorne viewed a deliberate isolation from one's fellows as a formula for spiritual disaster.

Related to the conflict which he thus experienced as a human being is a quite similar dichotomy stemming from his difficulties as an artist. Though primarily a portrayer of the moral picturesque, Hawthorne was aware that his tales lacked a sense of physical reality. He admitted that *The House of the Seven Gables* had "a great deal more to do with the clouds overhead than with any portion of the actual soil of the County of Essex" (III, 16). Earlier, in a letter to Longfellow, dated June 4, 1837, he referred to *Twice-Told Tales* and complained that he had "great difficulty, in the lack of materials; for I have seen so little of the world, that I have nothing but thin air to concoct my stories of, and it is not easy to give a life like semblance to such shadowy stuff." To provide himself with a repository of "side-scenes and backgrounds and exterior adornment" (Preface to *Our Old Home*, VII, 15) for insertion into his fiction, he began to compile his prolix and pedantic notebooks. They were to furnish the outer garments by means of which he hoped to endow his "shadows of imagination" with the semblance of materiality. His natural bent was toward "divestment," toward reducing the visibility of actual things; his constant efforts were directed toward "investment," toward outfitting the invisible with at least the trappings of reality. Yet the right balance between unsubstantiality and corporeality remained an elusive ideal. All his lifetime he made repeated attempts to bring to his romances a greater reality, without at the same time sacrificing too much of their primary abstract and metaphysical meaning. At times, and for certain chapters of his longer novels, he seems to have achieved what he was striving for. Mr.

Randall Stewart lists "Ethan Brand" and the account of
Zenobia's death in *The Blithedale Romance* as examples
of the few cases in point in which he managed to arrive
at a satisfactory proportion between the two extremes.[12]
But the conflict accruing to the artist in virtue of his
determination to strike the right mean remained unresolved.

Furthermore, speaking authorially in "The Artist of
the Beautiful," he made known his belief that "the ideal
artist [had] to possess a force of character that seems
hardly compatible with its delicacy; he must keep his
faith in himself while the incredulous world assails him
with its utter disbelief; he must stand up against mankind
and be his own sole disciple, both as respects his genius
and the objects to which it is directed" (II, 512).

As man and as artist, therefore, Hawthorne was subjected to a fourfold tension arising from an intensely
personal interest in the following problems:

1. which has the greater validity, intuition or understanding;
2. how overcome a tendency to aloofness without destroying
   one's individuality;
3. how mix the real with the ideal without sacrificing the
   ideal;
4. how develop at once forcefulness and delicacy of character.

He never completely resolved any one of the four.   But
the significant comment made in *Our Old Home,* and
referable primarily to his description of Litchfield Cathedral, is equally applicable here: ". . . it was something gained, even to have that painful sense of my own
limitations, and that half-smothered yearning to soar
beyond them" (VII, 154).

Conscious of his own difficulties, and decidedly empirical and subjective in his approach to metaphysics, Hawthorne's conception of man as a rational creature horribly at odds with himself was logical enough. His was, in fact, the same basic dichotomy which had motivated the thoughts and actions of his Puritan ancestors. For the Puritanism which the first of these ancestors professed consisted essentially in a double-edged paradox: "the abasement of man points to a supreme ideal of perfection, and the sense of a possible perfection makes man appear by contrast immeasurably abased." [13] Man, in other words, was a composite of spirit and matter. In virtue of the spiritual in him, he was possessed of measureless potentialities. In virtue of the material in him, he was doomed by his very composition never to realize his full potentialities. Were he to attempt to submerge the spiritual, and live on a purely animal level, the spiritual in him would rise to the surface to haunt him. Were he to become too acutely conscious of the high ideals to which he must aspire in virtue of the non-material in him, the purely material would soon force him to realize his limitations. Caught between God and the devil, he became a lone warrior on his own private battleground.

It is not unlikely, therefore, that Hawthorne's awareness of this seemingly irreconcilable split in man's nature may have been colored by his Puritan heritage, though constant introspection and a natural tendency to Paul Pry-ishness may have been of themselves sufficient to account for it. But no matter what factors contributed to its formation, it is certain that the New England writer was concerned almost to the point of obsession with this dichotomy in man, and with its various manifestations.

He found it operative in himself, as has been shown.

He found it symbolically present in Christ. Sodoma's Christ bound to the pillar, portraying His loneliness and despair as well as His awful majesty and grandeur, seemed almost to reconcile "an Omnipotent Divinity with a suffering and outraged humanity." [14]

He found it in his fellowmen. It was there he chose to study it—under various guises and beneath different aspects.

His notebooks are replete with concise plot outlines which might serve as a medium for analyzing more closely and probing more deeply this duality in man.

A person to consider himself as the prime mover of certain remarkable events, but to discover that his actions have not contributed in the least thereto.[15]

A man seeks for something excellent, and seeks it in the wrong way, and in a wrong spirit, and finds something horrible—as for instance, he seeks for treasure, and finds a dead body . . .[16]

A young man finds a portion of the skeleton of a Mammoth; he begins by degrees to become interested in completing it; searches round the world for the means of doing so; spends youth and manhood in the pursuit; and in old age has nothing to show for his life, but this skeleton.[17]

A benevolent person going about the world, and endeavoring to do good to every body; in pursuance of which object, for instance, he gives a pair of spectacles to a blind man—and does all such ill-suited things.[18]

In each of these four plot germs, the fundamental idea is the same: man attempts to achieve an ideal, but is foiled in his attempts. Whether he is foiled because of the sportive intervention of God, or because the end does not justify the means, or because of some radical deficiency in his nature is, for the moment at least, quite beside the point. Hawthorne was intensely conscious of the fact that even the best and noblest intentions of man might fail to realization, might, indeed, wreak havoc and tragedy.

Such, surely, is the moral of "The Birthmark," a full-length short story. Georgiana's blemish—the pigmy crimsoned mimic hand on her cheek—was the sole flaw in her beauty. Her scientist husband, Aylmer, intent upon achieving the ideal of absolute perfection, strove to remove this one remaining token of human imperfection. To that task he brought the vast resources of his laboriously accumulated scientific knowledge. He "aimed loftily"; he wrought "nobly"; the tint of the birthmark faded from the cheek; and Georgiana was dead.

In no other tale, and in none of his longer romances, does the fundamental dichotomy in man find such masterful expression. Nowhere did he probe more expertly the "almost giddy vertiginous gulf between human finiteness and the infinity of the Absolute." [19] A perusal of the large folio, in which Aylmer "had recorded every experiment in his scientific career, its original aim . . . and its final success" led Georgiana to observe "that his most splendid successes were almost invariably failures, if compared with the ideal at which he aimed." And this was so, even though the "physical details" in which he trafficked were redeemed "from materialism by his strong and eager aspiration towards the infinite." Hawthorne, speaking in his own right, referred to Aylmer's journal as "the sad confession and continual exemplification of the shortcomings of the composite man, the spirit burdened with clay and working in matter, and of the despair that assails the higher nature at finding itself so miserably thwarted by the earthly part" (II, 61 f.). The death of Georgiana assumes added significance in so far as it tends to show that only in death can man be freed of this "earthly part," only by dying can he even imperfectly bridge that "almost giddy vertiginous gulf."

Thus the shortcomings of the composite man destine

him for tragedy—for surely, Hawthorne implies, it is tragic that a noble and brilliant man should cause unhappiness and even death in his attempt to leap the chasm between potentiality and actuality.

He was perfectly aware, of course, that the composite nature of man does not always lead to tragedy on the Aylmer level. Had Georgiana been less beautiful—or had Aylmer been more of a clod and less of a genius— the tragedy need not have occurred. Tragedy on the Aylmer level occurs only when men become aware of the ideal, conscious of their possibilities.

4

It is precisely at this point that Hawthorne invites comparison with Herman Melville. Here, too, was a man who, largely through self-scrutiny, came to know about life "as a thing of sorrow and bitterness and frustration"; [20] for him, too, there were men so set at cross-purposes that they were destroyed—and destroyed others— "in the pursuit of their most noble intentions."

Tragedy, for Melville, results from the destruction of an ideal. But in order to destroy an ideal, it is absolutely necessary first of all to become conscious that there is an ideal. For the great majority of men, Melville would say, true tragedy—tragedy on the Aylmer level—is impossible, for the simple reason that they fail to take cognizance of the gap between what is and what could be—the gap between potentiality and actuality. That gulf is objectively real in every human being, since every human being is a composite of the spiritual and the material. But the mere fact that it exists is not enough. Most men are as unconscious of it as of the air they breathe. Only when they become subjectively aware of its existence, and strive to bridge it—only then do they become ripe for tragedy. For man can never bridge that gulf. Not the objective fact, therefore, but a too acute realization of the fact that the ideal exists and that it is beyond realization, at least in this life, makes for the tragedy that befalls Ahab and Pierre and Aylmer.

Basically, therefore, Hawthorne is in agreement with Melville. Aylmer is the true Melvillian tragic hero: an intellectual aristocrat who becomes conscious of the cleavage between what is and what ought to be, tries to mend it, and fails. Hawthorne, equally with Melville, held that the tragedy of Aylmer was ascribable, not to the existence of the cleavage, but to Aylmer's awareness of the cleavage coupled with his efforts to remedy it.

But Hawthorne departed from Melville in one important particular. Melville posited a tragic aristocracy: only the chosen few can be truly tragic, and tragedy, for him, is synonymous with grandeur. Hawthorne posited a tragic democracy: all men, though not all in equal measure, are tragic figures in the sense that the dichotomy is present in them all. And though they may not be aware of it, the duality in them is productive of consequences which have an objective reality. In other words, Hawthorne, unlike Melville, did not stress the awareness of the ideal. The tragedy is heightened when that awareness is present; but even without the awareness, the tragedy is still there, though in this latter case it might perhaps be more accurately termed frustration.

5

Hawthorne discovered hints and evidences of this frustration on all sides of him. "[It] is with children," he wrote, "as Mr[.] Emerson, or somebody else, says it is with nature [21]—you cannot see them so well when you look at them of set purpose. The best manifestations of them must take you at unawares." [22] He recorded a similar perversity in his own observations of nature.

I have before now experienced, that the best way to get a vivid impression and feeling of a landscape, is to sit down before it and read, or become otherwise absorbed in thought; for then, when your eyes happen to be attracted to the landscape, you seem to catch Nature at unawares, and see her before she has time to change her aspect.[23]

As with children and with nature, so too do the glories of architecture reveal themselves to those who do not go forth to find them. On a visit to St. Peter's Basilica, he noted that, occasionally, "a single, casual, momentary glimpse of its magnificence gleams upon my soul, as it were, when I happen to glance at arch opening beyond arch, and I am surprised into admiration when I least think of it. I have experienced that a landscape, and the sky, unfold their deepest beauty in a similar way, not when they are gazed at of set purpose, but when the spectator looks suddenly through a peep-hole among a crowd of other thoughts."[24]

Fourteen months later, he stood before Guido's picture of Beatrice Cenci. It, too, eluded a straightforward glance; it "can only be caught by side glimpses, or when the eye falls upon it casually, as it were, and without thinking to discover anything; as if the picture had a life and consciousness of its own, and were resolved not to betray its secret of grief or guilt, though it wears the full expression of it when it imagines itself unseen."[25]

Of themselves, such random remarks might be nothing more than casual commentaries on a somewhat unusual and purely personal phenomenon. But their frequent recurrence indicates that Hawthorne may have found them adumbrative of a more important aspect of men's lives. Just as one cannot achieve his most rewarding glimpses of children, nature, architecture, and painting when he goes forth of set purpose to get such glimpses, so, too, will true happiness elude that person who makes happiness an object of pursuit.

Happiness, in this world, if it comes at all, comes incidentally. Make it the object of pursuit, and it leads us a wild-
goose chase, and is never attained. Follow some other
object, and very possibly we may find that we have caught
happiness without dreaming of such luck; but, likely enough,
it is gone the moment we say to ourselves—'Here it is!'—
like the chest of gold that treasure-seekers find.[26]

Hawthorne's strong convictions on this point find varying expression. But however presented, the concept
behind them is always the same: man is a creature set
at cross-purposes in a world he did not create. He may
be granted brief glimpses of the glories of this creation—
but he will not get them on the strength of his determination, no matter how purposeful, to perceive these glories.
He may achieve happiness—but never if he makes it an
object of pursuit: ". . . happiness (which never comes
but incidentally) will come to us unawares" (*BR,* V,
472). For "the forms and appliances of human life are
never fit to make people happy, until they cease to be
used for the purposes for which they were directly intended, and are taken, as it were, in a sidelong application."[27] He can be sure, too, as Coverdale was, "that
the good we aim at will not be attained. People never
do get just the good they seek. If it comes at all, it is
something else, which they never dreamed of, and did
not particularly want" (*BR,* V, 406).

So, too, "many a noble race [has degenerated] . . . in
consequence of too strict a watchfulness to keep it pure"
(*HSG,* III, 296). Holgrave erred, Hawthorne told the
reader of *The House of the Seven Gables,* "in fancying
that it mattered anything to the great end in view [the
inauguration of a 'golden era'] whether he himself should
contend for it or against it" (III, 216). Hepzibah was
convinced that "whosoever, and with however kindly a
purpose, should come to help [her in her extremity], they
would be sure to help the strongest side!" (III, 289).

Governor Bellingham was not "ill fitted to be the head and representative of a community, which owed its origin and progress, and its present state of development, not to the impulses of youth, but to the stern and tempered energies of manhood, and the sombre sagacity of age; accomplishing so much, precisely because it imagined and hoped so little" (*SL,* V, 86).

Men are frustrated even in their pursuit of ignoble ends. Had it not been for Archbishop Laud's "persecution" of the Puritans, "New England would have remained long a wilderness, and at last have been settled by mere worldly adventurers, the most desperate of their generation, instead of the wisest and holiest." Thus error fights in the dark "and inflicts the heaviest blows on its own party in the battle; all its strength, as appears by the final result, goes to eke out the weakness of the adversary." [28] And in a letter to H. L. Conolly, dated June 17, 1850, Hawthorne told Conolly he actually did him a favor in having him dismissed from the surveyorship; had he not done so, there would have been no *Scarlet Letter.*

Always the sense of frustration! It is disastrous to perpetuate ancient systems and time-honored traditions— so teaches *The House of the Seven Gables.* But it is just as disastrous to abandon long-standing institutions and substitute for them the novel projects of the moment— such is the lesson of *The Blithedale Romance.*

Somewhere—elusive, like a will-o'-the-wisp—there is the ideal. That which is the spiritual in man makes him aware of it, even forces him at times to seek it out. But that which is the material in man urges him to be the realist, even proves to him that the perfect attainment of the ideal is impossible so long as man is part spiritual, part material. The ruins of Furness Abbey, Hawthorne was sure, "suggest a greater majesty and beauty than any human work can show—the crumbling traces of the half

obliterated design producing somewhat of the effect of
the first idea of anything admirable, when it dawns upon
the mind of an artist or poet—an idea, which, do what
he may, he is sure to fall short of." [29]

The author-observer of *The Blithedale Romance* was
equally convinced that any vision "worth the having
. . . is certain never to be consummated otherwise than
by a failure" (V, 332).

There can be no doubt, then, that Nathaniel Hawthorne viewed the life of man as beset on all sides by
frustrations. He is doomed by the antecedent factor of
composition never to realize, in this life, the potentialities
of which he is possessed in virtue of his having a soul.
Aylmer's failure was a classic case in point. "Thus
ever," Hawthorne added, "does the gross fatality of earth
exult in its invariable triumph over the immortal essence
which, in this dim sphere of half development, demands
the completeness of a higher state" (II, 69).

6

More often than not, convictions such as these would
have driven their possessor into the arms of a pessimistic
determinism. Had this possibility been realized, Hawthorne might well have become a name synonymous with
the literature of moral despair.

But his is not that brand of literature. Despite all the
frustrations—and the ensuing restlessness in man—he
dare not lose faith either in himself or in the ideal. Certainly, any vision worth the having is sure never to be
consummated otherwise than by failure. But "what of
that? Its airiest fragments, impalpable as they may be,
will possess a value that lurks not in the most ponderous
realities of any practicable scheme. They are not the
rubbish of the mind. Whatever else I may repent of,
therefore, let it be reckoned neither among my sins nor

follies that I once had faith and force enough to form generous hopes of the world's destiny,—yes! and to do what in me lay for their accomplishment; even to the extent of quitting a warm fireside, flinging away a freshly lighted cigar, and travelling far beyond the strike of city clocks, through a drifting snowstorm" (*BR,* V, 332). To strive for an elusive ideal, a far-fetched what-might-be, is to be a fool! Again, Hawthorne's answer, spoken through the mouth of Coverdale, is a blunt "So what?" "The greatest obstacle to being heroic is the doubt whether one may not be going to prove one's self [*sic*] a fool; the truest heroism is to resist the doubt; and the profoundest wisdom to know when it ought to be resisted, and when to be obeyed" (*BR,* V, 331). It is significant that there are times when the doubt should be resisted.

Holgrave, too, was wrong in supposing "that it mattered anything to the great end in view whether he should contend for it or against it." But it was well and good that he should think it mattered a great deal. For his enthusiasm, "infusing itself through the calmness of his character, and thus taking an aspect of settled thought and wisdom, would serve to keep his youth pure, and make his aspirations high. And when, with the years settling down more weightily upon him, his early faith should be modified by inevitable experience, it would be with no harsh and sudden revolution of his sentiments. He would still have faith in man's brightening destiny, and perhaps love him all the better, as he should recognize his helplessness in his own behalf; and the haughty faith, with which he began life, would be well bartered for a far humbler one at its close, in discerning that man's best directed effort accomplishes a kind of dream, while God is the sole worker of realities" (*HSG,* III, 216).

In fact, Hawthorne might well go so far as to say that man's greatest danger lies, not in an awareness of the chasm between the ideal and the real, as Melville maintained, but in the practical admission that the chasm can never be bridged. That was the tragedy of "poor and fallen Owen Warland [who] . . . had lost faith in the invisible, and now prided himself, as such unfortunates invariably do, in the wisdom which rejected much that even his eye could see, and trusted confidently in nothing but what his hand could touch. This is the calamity of men whose spiritual part dies out of them and leaves the grosser understanding to assimilate them more and more to the things of which alone it can take cognizance . . ." (II, 525). Such, too, was the tragedy of Deacon Drowne, the carver, for "who can doubt that the very highest state to which a human spirit can attain, in its loftiest aspirations, is its truest and most natural state, and that Drowne was more consistent with himself when he wrought the admirable figure of the mysterious lady, than when he perpetrated a whole progeny of blockheads?" (II, 362) And one of Hawthorne's earliest projected works, *The Story Teller,* was intended to serve as a warning to the reader "to adopt some great and serious aim, such as manhood will cling to, that he may not feel himself, too late, a cumberer of this overladen earth, but a man among men." [30] That this "great and serious aim" was certain never to be consummated otherwise than by failure was quite beside the point.

Calmly, almost dispassionately, therefore, Hawthorne promulgated the paradoxical doctrine that, though man is so constituted as never to achieve his loftiest aspirations, he dare not falter in his pursuit of the ideal.

7

Hawthorne did not concern himself with what lay behind this strange paradox. Unlike Melville, he felt no inner compulsion to speculate on what it was that subjected man to this constant frustration. He accepted the situation for what it was, and with restrained disillusion acknowledged its inexplicability.

Yet even while admitting its inexplicability, Hawthorne gave indications of having gone beyond the surface manifestations of the problem. Aylmer, he suggested authorially in the final lines of "The Birthmark," might have spared himself his great loss had he only adopted the long-range view, had he only taken up his position at a distance and attempted to see the total design. But the "momentary circumstance was too strong for him; he failed to look beyond the shadowy scope of time, and, living once for all in eternity, to find the perfect future in the present" (II, 69).

In his last years, too, he seemed not as certain as he once had been that the highest and noblest intentions of men invariably miscarry. In the body of an essay, "Chiefly about War Matters," he reiterated his often expressed opinion that no "human effort, on a grand scale, has ever yet resulted according to the purpose of its projectors. The advantages are always incidental. Man's accidents are God's purposes. We miss the good we sought, and do the good we little cared for." Yet in a footnote reference unmistakably written by himself, he denied, or at least questioned, the validity of this statement. That footnote reads: "The author seems to imagine that he has compressed a great deal of meaning into these little, hard, dry pellets of aphoristic wisdom. We disagree with him. The counsels of wise and good men are often coincident with the purposes of Providence, and the present war promises to illustrate our remark" (XII, 332).

It is entirely probable, of course, that the recantation was added purely as a sop to the New England abolitionists, and in no way indicated a departure from Hawthorne's well established thought trend. His letter to

Henry Bright, written on March 8, 1863, lends credence
to this view: "I never did really approve of the war,
though you may have supposed so from the violence and
animosity with which I controverted your notions about
it, when I wrote last. . . . if I have any wishes on the
subject, it is that New England might be a nation by
itself." Despite this adminicular evidence, however, it
is equally probable that Hawthorne was resorting to the
device of dividing his insights between the body of the
essay and its footnote, just as he was fond of dividing his
insights among the various characters of his novels.

But no matter what importance is finally attributed to
this puzzling phenomenon in the essay referred to, it
can safely be maintained that Hawthorne, if hard pressed
to commit himself, would have invoked once again his
unswerving belief in the inscrutability of the Creator's
designs. Difficulties and tensions and frustrations tell a
tale of man's restlessness—until the heart of man comes
to rest in God. That was Augustine's belief centuries
before it became Hawthorne's. And this belief of the
New England novelist, that God's designs, no matter
how haphazard and unjust they may appear to finite intellects, are nevertheless wise and good, accounts, it
seems to me, for the quiet and restraint with which Hawthorne clothes his record of man's frustrations.

Melville, except in *Billy Budd,* found such restraint
impossible. Driven by his temperament to try to fathom
the Absolute, he found himself floundering helplessly in
a dark and turbulent swamp. Descending ever deeper
and deeper into the cavern of his heart, which soon became for him co-extensive with the universe, he found
only blackness at the center of life. Hawthorne, too,
knew these depths of the human heart. In fact, he early
projected a story revolving about that very idea.

The human Heart to be allegorized as a cavern; at the
entrance there is sunshine, and flowers growing about it.

You step within, but a short distance, and begin to find yourself surrounded with a terrible gloom, and monsters of divers
kinds; it seems like Hell itself. You are bewildered, and
wander long without hope. At last a light strikes upon you.
You peep towards it, and find yourself in a region that
seems, in some sort, to reproduce the flowers and sunny
beauty of the entrance, but all perfect. These are the depths
of the heart, or of human nature, bright and peaceful; the
gloom and terror may lie deep; but deeper still is the eternal
beauty.[31]

The gloom and terror lie deep—as Melville found. But
Melville had to wait for *Billy Budd* to discover that
"deeper still is the eternal beauty." Hawthorne had less
difficulty than Melville in sounding the depths at which
lies eternal beauty because he entered the cavern convinced that somewhere beneath the darkness and gloom
lay God's incomprehensible wisdom and goodness.

Miriam, Hilda, and Kenyon, in one of their numerous
tours of Rome, visited what might have been the spot
"where the chasm opened, into which Curtius precipitated his good steed and himself." The Italian night and
the legendary air of the Forum made it easy to imagine
"the great, dusky gap, impenetrably deep, and with half-
shaped monsters and hideous faces looming upward out
of it, to the vast affright of the good citizens who peeped
over the brim!" Kenyon said he would give much for a
peep into the chasm.

"I fancy," remarked Miriam, "that every person takes
a peep into it in moments of gloom and despondency;
that is to say, in his moments of deepest insight. . . .
The firmest substance of human happiness is but a thin
crust spread over it, with just reality enough to bear up
the elusive stage-scenery amid which we tread" (*MF*, VI,
191 f.).

Hawthorne would have agreed—with an important
reservation. Beneath the crust of human happiness do
indeed lie gloom and despondency. Man's moments of

deeper insight are those in which he sees the darkness and frustration beneath the camouflage of happiness. But his moments of deepest insight are those in which he penetrates beyond the blackness, to discover that "deeper still is the eternal beauty."

Thus there are three successive stages to a mature resolution of life's frustrations: crack the outer shell of natural bliss, peer through the gloom and darkness, and pass beyond it to the core. Viewed from this central position, the gloom and darkness do not, it is true, disappear, but they do assume their rightful proportions.

This procedure is exemplified in "The Maypole of Merry Mount," particularly in its final paragraph.

And Endicott, the severest Puritan of all who laid the rock foundation of New England, lifted the wreath of roses from the rim of the Maypole, and threw it, with his own gauntleted hand, over the heads of the Lord and Lady of May. It was a deed of prophecy. As the moral gloom of the world [second stage] over-powers all systematic gayety [first stage], even so was their home of wild mirth [first stage] made desolate amid the sad forest [second stage]. They returned to it [the sad forest] no more [third stage]. But as their flowery garland was wreathed of the brightest roses that had grown there, so, in the tie that united them, were intertwined all the purest and best of their early joys. They went heavenward, supporting each other along the difficult path which it was their lot to tread, and never wasted one regretful thought on the vanities of Merry Mount (I, 84).

The crowning moments of *The Scarlet Letter* record the end of a similar journey. Earlier in the story, Hester and the minister had considered the possibility of flight, in order that they might have a happiness hitherto denied them. But this vision of natural bliss [first stage] disappeared. They returned to the village, Hester to walk publicly among the citizens of the town, arrayed as always in the scarlet letter, Dimmesdale to his hour of

public confession [second stage].   And in the final minutes of his ignominy, with the worst of the gloom and
darkness already behind him, he knows that "this [which
is to follow—the third stage—is far] better than what we
dreamed of in the forest" (V, 300).

Hawthorne's firm conviction that deep beneath the
conflicts and frustrations of life burns the light of beauty
can only be based on his belief that God's inscrutable
designs, incomprehensible though they be to the finite
mind of man, are nevertheless good and wise.   This conviction, whenever it occurs, is tantamount to an admission that man's lack of knowledge and understanding
must be supplemented by a trusting and unswerving reliance on the goodness and mercy of God.   Such a conviction, and its accompanying personal peace of mind,
can come only to one who adheres to the Augustinian
docta ignorantia.   For when self-reliance fails, and man
sees himself as finite, then piety waxes strong.   And in
so far as Hawthorne penetrated beneath the outer wrap-
pings of natural bliss and moral tension, to see beneath
them both the workings of a wise Providence, he translated into empirical truth the Puritan doctrine of God's
awful sovereignty.   At the same time, he refuted the
contention of those who, like William Peirce Randel,
were to say that from "established evidence it is clear
that at heart he was practically a skeptic." [32]   Hawthorne
was not a skeptic: he answered with a firm negative the
question posed years later by Thomas Hardy:

> Has some Vast Imbecility,
> Mighty to build and blend,
> But impotent to tend,
> Framed us in jest, and left us now to hazardry?

From what has already been said, it is quite clear that
Nathaniel Hawthorne was not inclined to obscure the
distinction between God and man. His theology was
theology properly so called; he did not posit an apotheo-
sized, infinitely perfectible man, and make him the subject of his theology.

Nor did he go to the other extreme and obliterate the
distinction between man and animal. There is, as he
put it, "one great and invariable mark of distinction between the Man with a soul, and the Animal without one.
The latter cannot communicate his intelligence to succeeding generations, nor accumulate it from age to age;
there is no progressive development of the intellect of
the race. It is otherwise with Man . . . he is capable
of adding wisdom to wisdom . . ."[33]

Man, therefore, has a soul. The animal does not.
That surely is a basic difference. Hawthorne, admittedly, beclouds the issue by attributing to animals as
well as to men an intelligence, though of a higher order
in the one case than in the other. However, the intellect is a power that resides in the soul alone. Therefore,
since animals have no souls, it is somewhat difficult to
understand how they can possess intellects, even of an
inferior order. Hawthorne, of course, was never interested in philosophical niceties, and may be conforming
himself to the lay view which rarely distinguishes between intelligence and instinct.

It is evident, too, from the passage just quoted, that
man is a creature composed of body and soul. Hawthorne's eschatology, coupled with his clear reference
to men as "spirits still embodied," [34] leaves no doubt as
to his position on this point. "We do wrong to our departed friends," he wrote in *The American Magazine of
Useful and Entertaining Knowledge*, "and clog our own

heavenward aspirations, by connecting the idea of the grave with that of death. Our thoughts should follow the celestial soul, and not the earthly corpse." [35] Man's composite nature is here once again clearly indicated: he is part soul, part body.

Nowhere does Hawthorne specifically state that the soul is the source of man's essence as well as of all of man's acts. Nor does he declare that the unmixed powers of the soul are intellect and will. In fact, he does not note the distinction between acts which proceed from powers residing in the soul and body together and acts which issue from powers lodged in the soul alone. But he does hold that man is possessed of intellect and free will; and since the body separated from the soul is capable neither of understanding nor willing, these powers must reside in the soul.

That man is a reasoning creature is a truth so evident that Hawthorne does not explicitly allude to it. Rather, he assumes it in such statements as the one already referred to. Man, he says, "is capable of adding wisdom to wisdom, throughout Eternity . . ."

But Hawthorne's position on the doctrine of free will has repeatedly come under fire. Commentators are by no means in agreement on the matter, some of them deducing an argument from the fact that he was predominantly a child of the Puritans, and therefore, as such, a predestinarian Calvinist.

Yet this argument, abstracting now from its initial lack of logic, is based on the assumption that the New England Puritans actually believed in absolute predestination, and consequently denied free will and human responsibility. The *Mayflower* pilgrims, it is true, may have held this belief. But almost from the very beginning there was a pronounced tendency to reinterpret the doctrines of Calvin in terms of the so-called Covenant Theology. God, in other words, was less arbitrary than the *Institutes* had made Him. He had, in fact, freely surrendered to a code of equity; any person who sincerely and practically believed in God would receive grace sufficient unto salvation.

Numbered among these Covenant theologians were such respected New Englanders as Thomas Shepard of Cambridge, Peter Bulkeley of Concord, and the compiler of Puritan theology, Samuel Willard. It is not apropos to the purpose at hand to trace the growth of this radical departure from the dogmas of John Calvin. But the shift from piety to moralism, extending over a period of a century and a half, is responsible in large part for the decline of a pristine New England Puritanism. By piety is to be understood that frame of mind which simply accepts the supposition that no one can be saved except by God's grace, and that this grace is conferred arbitrarily and independently of one's merits. Moralism implies that man can, to some extent, work out his own salvation, that he is himself responsible for his own damnation or salvation, as the case may be. The shift from piety to moralism found its final expression in Channing's famous Baltimore sermon of 1819, and in the formation of the American Unitarian Association in 1825.

In the light of this basic deviation from New England orthodoxy, it is clear that Hawthorne's heritage may as readily be labeled Unitarian (or Arminian) as Puritan. And since the milieu in which he lived and wrote was predominantly one in which men believed in, and lived as though they possessed, free will; since furthermore, the doctrine of free will had been in the ascendancy for more than four generations prior to his birth, it seems highly tenuous to deduce any *a priori* argument from his being a child of the Puritans.

A second series of arguments purporting to show that Hawthorne did not subscribe to the doctrine of free volitional acts arises from his frequent use of such terms as

fate, destiny, dark necessity, doom. The proponents of
this approach remember that Roger Chillingworth told
Hester: "By thy first step awry thou didst plant the germ
of evil; but since that moment, it has all been dark necessity" (V, 210). Obviously, though, there is no indication that Chillingworth here is voicing Hawthorne's personal belief. Nor is it quite clear why the latter portion
of the statement should be given more prominence than
the former, in which "the first step awry" is spoken of as
a free act. Hawthorne, of course, does use the terms
fate and *destiny*: the exact meaning of such words, however, must be determined from the context and in the
light of the author's total thought regarding the doctrine
of God's providence. Such an examination has already
been made;[36] the conclusions arrived at there do not
justify the contention that Hawthorne was a determinist.

Furthermore, the New England author looked upon
man as a free agent. The actions of his characters, albeit
with some obvious exceptions, would be meaningless,
were it not for the fact that their deeds entail a certain
moral culpability—and moral culpability is possible only
if the will of man is free. Hester, for example, commits
a sin in not informing Dimmesdale of Chillingworth's
identity. There is no indication that she was in any way
forced to keep that knowledge from the minister; the
mere fact that she later repented and divulged his identity is proof of her freedom to do or not to do. Dimmesdale, too, rises above his meaner self, accepts God's
grace, and confesses his sin. Hawthorne's preoccupation
with sin and its consequences is utterly meaningless, if
free will and human responsibility are but a mirage!
Trees and rocks, lacking free will, are capable neither
of sin nor of repentance; man alone can commit sin, and
he can do so only if his will is free.

Not only in his tales and romances, but in his letters
and journals as well, Hawthorne gives clear evidence of

his position on this point. In a letter to G. S. Hillard, dated January 20, 1850, he confesses that something else besides pride "teaches me that ill-success in life is really and justly a matter of shame. . . . The fault of a failure is attributable—in a great degree at least—to the man who fails." Surely there is explicit here the denial that man is predetermined to success or failure.

A similar denial is implicit in his comments on man's posthumous reputation. "What nonsense it is, this care of ours for good fame or bad fame after death! If it were of the slightest real moment, our reputations would have been placed by Providence more in our own power, and less in other people's, than they now are." [37]

Less than a year before his death, he wrote to Samuel H. Emery, Jr., defending himself against the charge of having deliberately maligned the "reverend clergy." In the course of the letter, dated November 6, 1863, he restated the true moral of the offending sketch, namely, "that no man is safe from sin and disgrace till by divine assistance he has thoroughly cleansed his heart—which few of us take the pains to do, though many satisfy themselves with a shallow and imperfect performance of that duty." Certainly, this constitutes a clear affirmation of man's freedom: he, not God, though God grants assistance, must cleanse his heart; and if but few men take the pains to do it, then it is surely within man's power to take those pains.

Purely authorial comments throughout the novels corroborate these conclusions. The author-observer of *The Blithedale Romance* listened with "horror and disgust" to accounts "of the miraculous [mesmeric] power of one human being over the will and passions of another," for he saw that, "if these things were to be believed, the individual soul was virtually annihilated . . . and . . . the idea of man's eternal responsibility was made ridiculous . . . But I would have perished on the spot sooner than believe it" (V, 544 f.).

In the Capitol at Rome is to be seen "a symbol (as apt at this moment as it was two thousand years ago) of the Human Soul, with its choice of Innocence or Evil close at hand, in the pretty figure of a child, clasping a dove to her bosom, but assaulted by a snake" (*MF*, VI, 19). Here, too, Hawthorne, speaking for himself, specifically attributes to man the powers of a free agent, though it should be noted that the reference in this last passage is to a freedom of exercise rather than to a freedom of specification.

All the evidence, then, points in one direction: man's will is free and undetermined.

9

Hawthorne's views on the nature of the human soul, as these are deducible from his works, scarcely warrant a systematic treatment. It is legitimate to assume that from his knowledge of the soul's non-materiality he would have inferred its spirituality. Likewise, from the same fact of non-materiality, he might have inferred its simplicity. And from its simplicity, in turn, he could have deduced its incorruptibility.

Hawthorne, of course, was not interested in such a chain of logical inferences. But one aspect of the soul's nature engrossed him from beginning to end of his writing: the soul's immortality.

That the soul is immortal appears from many a passage of Hawthorne's works, even though an isolated statement here and there may seem to prove the contrary. Commenting, for example, on the grandeur of the Swiss landscape, he wrote that its beauty was "more than enough for poor, perishable mortals." [38] In *The American Magazine of Useful and Entertaining Knowledge* he expressed an editorial wish to "be buried as our father's [*sic*] were. We desire to give mortality its own. Our clay must not be baulked of its repose. We are willing to let it moulder beneath the little hillock, and that the sods should gradually settle down, and leave no traces of our grave. . . . what belongs to earth, let the earth take." [39]

With the same editorial assurance, however, he found it possible to issue this warning: ". . . whatever may be the duration of this earthly existence, let it ever be in our minds, that another comes hastening on—which is eternal." [40]   Authorially, he could speak of the "infant immortality" [Pearl] committed to Hester's charge (*SL,* V, 116).

The apparent contradiction in these two groups of statements vanishes in the light of Hawthorne's concept of man as a composite of body and soul, of the spiritual and the material.   The body, as he well knew, will "moulder beneath the little hillock," but the soul, the form of the body, in the Aristotelian sense of the word *form,* lives on in another existence.

Of this Hawthorne is quite sure.   A perfect day, he recorded in his notebooks, is the promise of a blissful eternity; "our Creator would never have made such weather, and have given us the deep hearts to enjoy it above and beyond all thought, if He had not meant us to be immortal." [41]   On the occasion of his mother's death his reasoning took a different turn.   The conclusion drawn, however, was the same.

Oh what a mockery, if what I saw were all,—let the interval between extreme youth and dying age be filled with what happiness it might!   But God would not have made the close [of life] so dark and wretched, if there were nothing beyond; for then it would have been the fiend that created us, and measured out our existence, and not God.   It would be something beyond wrong—it would be insult—to be thrust out of life into annihilation in this miserable way.   So, out of the very bitterness of death, I gather the sweet assurance of a better state of being. [42]

Not only "the very bitterness of death," but all of life itself points to an existence after death. "God himself," he believed, "cannot compensate us for being born, in any period short of eternity. All the misery we endure here constitutes a claim for another life;—and, still more, all the happiness, because all true happiness involves something more than the earth owns, and something more than a mortal capacity for the enjoyment of it." [43]

Nor was Hawthorne content to rest in the simple assurance that, by every law of logic, there should be an existence after death. There actually was. Robert Raikes, the founder of the Sunday School system, Hawthorne wrote, "has now been long dead. . . . And we may be permitted to believe that, in the celestial world, where the founder of the system now exists, he has often met with other happy spirits, who have blessed him as the earthly means by which they were rescued from hopeless ignorance and evil, and guided on the path to heaven." [44] The proof value of this statement is enhanced by the parenthetical casualness with which this man's existence in the celestial world is assumed rather than stressed. Likewise, in a letter of condolence [dated April 26, 1855] to a friend, Horatio Bridge, written upon the death of the latter's daughter, Hawthorne expressed the hope that "some time or other . . . you will be able to feel that, though it is good to have a dear child on earth, it is likewise good to have one safe in heaven. She will await you there . . ."

10

Nathaniel Hawthorne's definition of a person, even if he had seriously attempted one, would have little *verbal* correspondence with the classic definition of Boethius: a person is "an individual substance of a rational nature." [45]   Implicit in that Boethian formulation of the concept *person* are three basic truths:

1. man is a substance, capable of supporting himself;
2. man is an individual, unable to share with another the perfection of his subsistence;
3. man is endowed with reason and free will.

Now from the fact that man is endowed—Hawthorne would add, by Almighty God—with reason and free will, it follows that he is the master of his life and destiny. It follows, too, that "his being is a shrine and a holy of holies which is strictly his own, into which no one, except his Creator, can enter." [46]   For since man is a free agent, he is something "sacred and inviolable," possessed of inalienable rights and responsibilities.

Writing to Sophia Peabody, on October 18, [1841], he warned her against submitting herself to the mesmeric influence of another in the hope of obtaining relief from recurrent attacks of headache. "If I possessed such a power over thee," he told her, "I should not dare to exercise it; nor can I consent to its being exercised by another. Supposing that this power arises from the transfusion of one spirit into another, it seems to me that the sacredness of an individual is violated by it; there would be an intrusion into thy holy of holies . . ." Philosophically, of course, Hawthorne's supposition of a possible "transfusion of one spirit into another" is untenable: that which makes a person a person is incommunicable. Nevertheless, this letter to Miss Peabody is evidence of his high regard for "the sacredness of an individual."

So sacred, in fact, did Hawthorne consider the human person that his concept of an "unpardonable sin" is inextricably bound up with the failure to respect this inviolability. Various entries in his American notebooks, extending over a period of six years (1838-1844),[47] chart the gradual development of his thought on the

subject of an "unpardonable sin." His final entry concerning the matter is almost a summary of his conclusions: "The Unpardonable Sin might consist in a want
of love and reverence for the Human Soul; in consequence of which, the investigator pried into its dark
depths . . . from a cold philosophical curiosity . . ." [48]

This germinal idea was corporeally presented in the
characters of some of Hawthorne's major villains. Chillingworth was accused by Dimmesdale of a blacker sin
than adultery: for he "violated, in cold blood, the sanctity of a human heart" (V, 234). Ethan Brand had
made the girl Esther "the subject of a psychological experiment, and wasted, absorbed, and perhaps annihilated
her soul, in the process" (III, 489). Dr. Rappaccini
made Beatrice and Giovanni the subjects of his experi-
ments. Matthew Maule mesmerized Alice Pyncheon in
order to learn the location of a lost document. Westervelt mesmerized Priscilla, for no other reason than to
enhance his theatrical reputation.

In every case, the purpose to be achieved through the
exercise of such scientific or mesmeric powers was different. But all five violated the sacredness of the individual
because they were guilty of subordinating the human
person to an end for which it was never intended. In so
doing, they interfered with the inherent right of man to
be the master of his own life and destiny. Hawthorne
was willing to admit that the Faustian temptation to ac-
quire "empire over the human spirit" is a very grave one.
This temptation Holgrave resisted. And Holgrave's
creator paid his daguerrotypist the distinguished compli-
ment of conceding to him "the rare and high quality of
reverence for another's individuality" (*HSG,* III, 253).

Thus Hawthorne's concern for the sanctity of the human personality, as expressed in his censure of those
who violate that sanctity as well as in his praise of those
who reverence it, is abundant and final proof of his be-

lief that man is a free agent. For man is sacred and inviolable precisely because he comes from the hands of his Creator outfitted with a will that is free—so free that "God Himself cannot make him a mere instrument except by man's own will." [49]

11

Professor Perry Miller has described the Puritans as "scholastics with everything omitted that seemed to support the Papacy; they believed that they had purified medieval learning of its abuses, and therefore saw no reason why it should not be retained and adopted as their own." [50]

If that is true, then Hawthorne, in so far as his views concerning the rational creature man are concerned, has purified the Puritans. His basic beliefs: that man is composed of body and soul; that in his soul reside the powers of intellect and free will; that in virtue of his free will he is constituted a person sacred and inviolable; that he is destined for a life beyond this life—these beliefs are all in the true Aristotelian-Thomistic tradition. In his staunch insistence upon man's free will, as well as in his conviction that man is deprived rather than depraved, he departs from orthodox Calvinistic Puritanism. In his insistence upon man's frustrations he is perhaps more Platonic and Augustinian than Aristotelian and Thomistic. And in his failure to take formal cognizance of man's final destiny he is a humanitarian. But the pillars and rafters of the structure remain essentially Scholastic.

NOTES

[1] Jacques Maritain, *Three Reformers* (New York: Charles Scribner's Sons [n. d.]), p. 144.

[2] *Ibid.*, pp. 231 f.

[3] Fulton J. Sheen, *Philosophy of Religion* (New York: Appleton-Century-Crofts, Inc., 1948), p. 348.

[4] *Ibid.*, p. 350.

[5] Reinhold Niebuhr, *Nature and Destiny of Man,* I, 3 f.

[6] Norman Holmes Pearson, *The College Years of Nathaniel Hawthorne* (New Haven: Yale University, unpublished, 1932), p. 88.

[7] *The French and Italian Notebooks,* III, 495.

[8] *The English Notebooks,* p. 349.

[9] Herbert W. Schneider, *A History of American Philosophy* (New York: Columbia University Press, 1946), p. 143.

[10] Darrell Abel, "Hawthorne's Ethics" (Unpublished Ph.D. dissertation, Department of English, University of Michigan, 1948), p. 85.

[11] Pearson, *op. cit.,* p. 78.

[12] *The American Notebooks,* p. xliii.

[13] Miller, *op. cit.,* p. 45.

[14] *The French and Italian Notebooks,* III, 616.

[15] *Passages from the American Note-Books,* IX, 27.

[16] *The American Notebooks,* p. 101.

[17] *Ibid.*

[18] *Ibid.*, p. 125.

[19] Herbert Read, "Hawthorne," *Hound and Horn,* III (January-March, 1930), 217.

[20] Stanley Geist, *Herman Melville: The Tragic Vision and the Heroic Ideal* (Cambridge, Massachusetts: Harvard University Press, 1939), p. 19. The approach to Melville adopted in this study is worked out in full detail by Mr. Geist in this monograph.

[21] *Emerson's Complete Works* (Cambridge, 1883), I, 25.

[22] *The American Notebooks,* p. 199. Cf. also *ibid.,* p. 201.

[23] *Ibid.*, pp. 241 f. Cf. also *The English Notebooks,* II, 254 f.

[24] *The French and Italian Notebooks,* II, 114.

[25] *Ibid.*, III, 652.

[26] *The American Notebooks,* p. 140. Cf. also *The Blithedale Romance,* V, 472.

[27] *The English Notebooks,* p. 484.

[28] *The American Magazine of Useful and Entertaining Knowledge* (April, 1836), as quoted in Turner, *op. cit.,* p. 236.

[29] *The English Notebooks,* p. 157.

[30] Nelson F. Adkins, "The Early Projected Works of Nathaniel Hawthorne," *Papers of the Bibliographical Society of America,* XXXIX (1945), 143. Cf. *Tales, Sketches, and Other Papers,* XII, 40.

[31] *The American Notebooks,* p. 98.

[32] William Peirce Randel, "Hawthorne, Channing, and Margaret Fuller," *American Literature,* X (January, 1939), 476.

[33] *The American Magazine of Useful and Entertaining Knowledge* (August, 1836), as quoted in Turner, *op. cit.,* pp. 209 f.

[34] *The American Notebooks,* p. 187.

[35] Quoted in Turner, *op. cit.,* p. 100.

[36] Cf. chapter I, section 5.

[37] *The English Notebooks,* p. 415.

[38] *The French and Italian Notebooks,* III, 700.

[39] Quoted in Turner, *op. cit.,* p. 90.

[40] *Ibid.,* p. 169.

[41] *The American Notebooks,* p. 188.

[42] *Ibid.,* p. 210.

[43] *The English Notebooks,* p. 101.

[44] Nathaniel Hawthorne, "A Good Man's Miracle," *The Child's Friend: designed for Families and Sunday Schools,* I (February, 1844), 156. Quoted in Norman Holmes Pearson, "A Sketch by Hawthorne," *The New England Quarterly,* VI (1933), 144.

[45] Boethius, *De Persona et Duabus Naturis,* Chapter III.

[46] Robert Edward Brennan, O.P., *The Image of His Maker* (Milwaukee: The Bruce Publishing Company, 1948), p. 270.

[47] *The American Notebooks,* pp. lxxii ff.

[48] *Ibid.,* p. 106.

[49] J. Messner, *Social Ethics,* trans. J. J. Doherty (St. Louis: B. Herder Book Co., 1949), p. 90.

[50] Miller, *op. cit.,* p. 105.

The wretched minister! . . . . Tempted by a dream of happiness, he had yielded himself, with deliberate choice, as he had never done before, to what he knew was deadly sin. And the infectious poison of that sin had been thus rapidly diffused throughout his moral system.

—*The Scarlet Letter,* V, 265.

I. THE NATURE OF SIN

Mr. Barriss Mills has called Hawthorne "the anatomist of sin." [1] The term is ill-chosen. An anatomist is one skilled in the art of dissecting, of separating various component parts of an object, in order to ascertain their position, relation, and function. Mere interest in and intuitive perception of a structure, be it material or otherwise, are not the distinguishing marks of an anatomist.

Nathaniel Hawthorne was, by temperament and training, incapable of the scientific approach one rightly demands of the true analyst. This deficiency in method in no way minimizes the importance of his contribution to the record of man's thinking on the problem of sin. But it does render any attempt to arrive at a certain and systematic formulation of his views extremely hazardous.

In view of this antecedent difficulty, a brief account of the common teaching of Christianity on the concept of sin will prove useful.

The main tradition of the Christian Church has never departed from the Augustinian belief that in the human will itself lies the ultimate source of moral evil. Nor does the fact that God Himself gave man free will make God responsible for moral evil. In his treatise *On Free Will,* St. Augustine takes full cognizance of this very objection. The will, he answers in effect, is a good conferred by Almighty God; had He not bestowed this boon, man would be incapable of righteous action, a circumstance which, to the mind of Augustine, is inconceivable. Now the capacity for right action involves the capacity for wrong action. But God, since He is supremely good, can be neither the source of evil nor responsible for evil. The only other possible source is man himself. "So true is it that every sin is voluntary, that unless it be voluntary, it is no sin at all." [2]

Furthermore, St. Augustine defines sin as "a word, deed, or desire, contrary to the eternal law." [3] This definition is defended and adopted by Thomas Aquinas.

. . . sin is nothing else than an evil human act. Now an act is a human act because it is voluntary . . . whether it be voluntary, as being elicited by the will, *e.g.,* to will or to choose, or as being commanded by the will, *e.g.,* the exterior actions of speech or operation. Again, a human act is evil through lacking conformity with its due measure. Now the conformity of measure in a thing depends on a rule, from which if that thing depart, it is without measure. But there are two rules of the human will: one is proximate and homogeneous, viz., the human reason; the other is the first rule, viz., the eternal law, which is God's reason, so to speak. Accordingly, Augustine includes two things in the definition of sin: one, pertaining to the substance of a human act, and which is, as it were, the matter of sin, when he says, *word, deed, or desire;* the other, pertaining to the nature of evil, and which is the form, as it were, of sin, when he says, *contrary to the eternal law.*[4]

The objects of the natural law, then—and the natural law is the participation in human reason of God's eternal law—are "all those actions which in themselves are conformable or not conformable to rational human nature."

They are actions which are necessarily prescribed because they are demanded by human nature, or, on the contrary, they are necessarily forbidden, because they are contrary to the demands of human nature. They are good or evil, not merely because they are commanded or forbidden by lawful authority, but because in themselves they are becoming or unbecoming for man to perform because human nature is what it is.[5]

Now this natural law must be applied to particular cases. That dictate or judgment of the practical reason which decides that a particular action is right or wrong is traditionally termed conscience. Conscience is, as the theologians express it, "the herald or ambassador of God to each individual, making known to him and applying the eternal law of God to the conduct of life." [6] This, of course, has never been interpreted to mean that the conscience of the individual is entirely autonomous. Moral theologians are quick to add that a right conscience will recognize the necessity of conforming to any properly constituted authority, particularly to the supreme authority of God, as expressed, for example, in positive divine law.

By way of preliminary recapitulation, therefore, sin may be defined as a voluntary transgression of the law of God. This law of God is embodied either in the dictates of right reason or in the commands of a legitimately constituted superior. Practically speaking, an action may be forbidden on both counts: murder, for example, is against right reason and against the law of the state. But it is important to note that to disobey the command of a legitimate superior is in itself against right reason and therefore against the law of God. Every sin, therefore, is *theological*, objectively and subjectively. Objectively, it is a transgression ultimately of a law of God. Subjectively, it implies that the sinner knows, albeit obscurely, that he is somehow subject to a Supreme Being who commands men to maintain right order and forbids them to violate that order.

That this right order has an objective validity is clear from the fact that it represents the will and command of God. Any transgression of this order, then, is a sin, objectively speaking; but it is what theologians call a *material sin*. This term is opposed to *formal sin,* which is the phrase traditionally employed to express the wilful and knowing transgression of God's law. For example, a native on the banks of the Yalu is convinced that he would show filial respect to a cancerous father if he were to kill him and thus rid him of his sufferings. Firmly believing in the righteousness of his contemplated action, he kills his father. In so doing, he commits the material sin of murder: objectively, he transgresses God's law; subjectively, however, he does not act willingly and knowingly counter to God's law. He therefore does not sin formally. In the accepted theological view, formal sins—and formal sins only—incur guilt in the sight of God, because only a voluntary transgression represents a rebellion against the eternal law of God.

Viewed in the light of this traditional Christian teaching on the nature of sin, Hawthorne's thinking shows correspondences and deviations. But it is impossible to begin the process of determining the precise import of these before one has definitely ascertained whether or not Hawthorne observes the distinction between cosmic (physical) evil and moral evil. This is a distinction consistently adhered to by Augustine, and, in fact, by anyone who has speculated fruitfully about the problem of evil. Yet it is a distinction which Hawthorne at times seems to ignore.

Writing in his notebook for October 25, 1836, he outlines plans for a "new classification of society" on the basis of men's sorrows, their maladies, their sins; having done this, he will "proceed to generalize and classify the whole world together, as none can claim utter exemption from sorrow, sin, or disease; and if they could, yet Death, like a great parent, comes and sweeps them all through one darksome portal,—all his children." [7] Hawthorne, in this passage, as well as in "The Procession of Life" (II, 235-252), fails to distinguish between sin and disease, or between sin and sorrow. It is true, of course, that either disease or sorrow may be the consequence of sin, but this benign interpretation seems scarcely justified by the context.

Similarly, in a sentence of purely authorial explanation, he remarks that the "perception of an infinite, shivering solitude, amid which we cannot come close enough to human beings to be warmed by them, and where they turn to cold, chilly shapes and mist, is one of the most forlorn results of any accident, misfortune, crime, or peculiarity of character, that puts an individual ajar with the world" (*MF*, VI, 138). Speaking editorially, he admits the possibility that "the nice action of the mind [may be] . . . set ajar by any violent shock, as of great misfortune or great crime, so that the finer perceptions may be blurred thenceforth, and the effect be traceable in all the minutest conduct of life" (*MF*, VI, 693).

Passages such as these—and they are not infrequent—tend to cast a shadow of doubt upon the conclusions drawn from any detailed examination of the Hawthornian concept of sin. For if moral evil and physical evil are essentially identical, if there is no differences between murder and an earthquake, then it is useless to speculate on Hawthorne's position. I do not imply that the passages in question prove the failure to make this all-important distinction; in fact, the difficulties inherent in them may be merely apparent, and may be resolved in the total pattern of his thinking on the subject. Fortunately, too, as will become apparent, there are passages, the validity of which for the present investigation cannot be controverted.

2

Nathaniel Hawthorne holds that the will of man is the cause of sin.

*   *   *   *   *

Dimmesdale and Hester had determined to leave New England, in order to seek shelter and concealment together in the Old World, presumably as man and wife. Commenting on this resolution, Hawthorne noted that the minister, "[t] empted by a dream of happiness . . . had yielded himself, with deliberate choice, as he had never done before, to what he knew was deadly sin" (*SL*, V, 265).

Moral theologians are unanimous in detailing three requisites for a mortal or deadly sin. These are:

1. a grievous matter;
2. a full knowledge of the evil;
3. a full consent of the will.

In the case presented above, all three requisites are fulfilled: adultery, or placing oneself into an occasion in which the sin of adultery is more than likely to be committed, is, in the moral code of Dimmesdale, a grievous matter; he had full knowledge of the evil, that is, he clearly knew it to be a deadly sin; and he had full consent of the will: Hawthorne wrote that he "had yielded himself, with deliberate choice . . ."

The supreme importance of this passage, however, lies in the fact that Dimmesdale never actually carried out his plans. He merely consented. Consent implies an act of the will. Yet that act of the will constituted a deadly sin, for Hawthorne added: "And the infectious poison of that sin had been . . . rapidly diffused throughout his moral system. It had stupefied all blessed impulses, and awakened into vivid life the whole brotherhood of bad ones. Scorn, bitterness, unprovoked malignity, gratuitous desire of ill, ridicule of whatever was good and holy, all awoke, to tempt, even while they frightened him" (V, 265).

The mere consent of the will—even though not realized in any physical act—is in itself and of itself a sin: that is Hawthorne's position. In fact, on this occasion Dimmesdale committed a sin far more grievous than the one of which he had been guilty when he actually committed adultery. This is quite clear from the consequences. Having consented to flight with Hester, he could scarcely refrain "from uttering [in the presence of the deacon] certain blasphemous suggestions that rose into his mind, respecting the communion supper" (V, 260). He could recall no text of Scripture which he might whisper into the "rapturously attentive ear" of the oldest female member of his church (V, 261). He was strongly tempted "to blight . . . the innocence" of a maiden newly won to the church by his own sermon (V, 262). He felt a strange impulse to "stop short in the road, and teach some very wicked words to a knot of little Puritan children who were playing there, and had just begun to talk" (V, 263). No such strange inclinations and temptations plagued him after his actual adultery with Hester. But they occurred now—because of a sin which consisted exclusively in an act of the will.

The reason is not far to seek. The latter sin, albeit solely in the will, was greater precisely because the minister on this occasion had full consent of the will—"he had yielded himself, with deliberate choice." The previous sin, we are told, "had been a sin of passion, not of principle, or even of purpose" (V, 240). Passion, a lack of purpose, of deliberation, diminish the voluntariness of an act and, consequently, too, the gravity of the sin.

It is difficult to overestimate the value of this key passage in any attempt to analyze Hawthorne's thinking on the nature of sin. So closely does the concept of sin contained therein parallel the common teaching of moral theologians through the ages that one is inclined to rest the case on this one piece of evidence alone. Yet to do so would be to lose sight of significant foliations in the author's thought.

In "Fancy's Show-Box," a "morality," Hawthorne set himself the task of deciding "whether the soul may contract such stains [of sin], in all their depth and flagrancy, from deeds which may have been plotted and resolved upon, but which, physically, have never had existence." An earthly tribunal, he well knew, could recognize none but perpetrated crimes. But will not guilty thoughts "draw down the full weight of a condemning sentence, in the supreme court of eternity"?

In the solitude of a midnight chamber or in a desert, afar from men, or in a church, while the body is kneeling, the soul may pollute itself even with those crimes which we are accustomed to deem altogether carnal. If this be true, it is a fearful truth (I, 250).

Having posed the problem, he proceeded to illustrate it by an imaginary example. Fancy, Memory, and Conscience collaborate to show a Mr. Smith that sinful thoughts, though never embodied in acts, may yet "give valid evidence against him at the day of judgment."

The demonstration finished, Hawthorne admitted that Mr. Smith "might have argued the matter with Conscience, and alleged many reasons wherefore she should not smite him so pitilessly." Assuming the role of attorney for the defense, he argued that "not until the crime is accomplished [does guilt clinch] . . . its gripe upon the guilty heart, and claims it for its own. . . . Let us hope, therefore, that all the dreadful consequences of sin will not be incurred, unless the act have set its seal upon the thought."

In a final paragraph, however, he apparently realized the inadequacy of his defense. "Man must not disclaim his brotherhood, even with the guiltiest, since, though his hand be clean, his heart has surely been polluted [stained] by the flitting phantoms of iniquity." Furthermore, man "must feel that, when he shall knock at the gate of heaven, no semblance of an unspotted life can entitle him to entrance there. Penitence must kneel, and Mercy come from the footstool of the throne, or that golden gate will never open!" (I, 257)

The problem posed at the outset of "Fancy's Show-Box" has now been resolved. Sinful thoughts, even though they never find fulfillment in acts, stain the heart. The soul "may pollute itself" even "while the body is kneeling" in a church. Penitence must follow such thoughts just as necessarily as it must follow guilty actions, for, in Hawthorne's reasoned belief, both are equally sinful.

It is pertinent to note that on June 25, 1834, Hawthorne borrowed from the Salem Athenaeum Library, Jeremy Taylor's *Ductor Dubitantium: or, The Rule of Conscience* (London, 1676).[8] Rule III, Part II, Book IV, Chapter I of this work is entitled "The act of the will alone, although no external action or event do follow, is imputed to good or evil by God and man." Jeremy Taylor maintains throughout that the morality of an action "depends wholly on the will, and is seated in the inner man."[9] Hawthorne, in the concluding lines of "Fancy's Show-Box," agreed with Taylor, though he had given serious thought to the alternative. Years later, in *The Scarlet Letter,* he had no further need to explore other possibilities. His position was clear: "so true is it that every sin is voluntary, that unless it be voluntary, it is no sin at all."

Of equal importance is Hawthorne's thinking on that requisite of sin commonly termed *a full knowledge of the evil.* Practically speaking, this simply means that no act, however wrong it may be objectively, will be imputed to man as sin unless he knows that what he is doing is sinful. This is the basis for the theological distinction between formal sin and material sin. And while Hawthorne made no use of the terminology, he was clearly conscious of the distinction.

John C. Gerber, in a very perceptive study of *The Scarlet Letter,* denies that there is any "such thing as uniformity in . . . [Hawthorne's] concept of sin."

To assume this [uniformity] is to confuse the characters and to misinterpret most of the speeches. Sin in *The Scarlet Letter* is a violation of only that which the sinner *thinks* he violates. To one character, adultery is a transgression against God's law, to another, no more than a violation of the natural order of things. . . . To speak, therefore, even of adultery or hypocrisy without discovering what they mean to each individual is to become hopelessly confused about what Hawthorne is doing.[10]

Mr. Gerber, in this excerpt from his article, loses sight of the fact that a "violation of the natural order of things" cannot but be a "transgression against God's law." Certainly, too, if, as he correctly says, sin "is a violation of only that which the sinner *thinks* he violates," then this in itself is a very basic uniformity in Hawthorne's concept of sin. For no one commits a sin unless he knows that what he is about to do is wrong, and, knowing this, willingly does it anyway.

For example, Hester as well as Dimmesdale agreed to leave New England and seek a joint happiness in the Old World. Yet Hawthorne did not record that she "yielded" herself, with deliberate choice, to what she "knew was deadly sin." Nor was she plagued with the various temptations which beset the minister. On the contrary, her sex, "her youth, and the whole richness of her beauty, came back from what men call the irrevocable past, and clustered themselves, with her maiden hope, and a happiness before unknown, within the magic circle of this hour" (*SL,* V, 243).

Now what is the difference between Dimmesdale's act of the will and Hester's act of the will? Objectively, there is no difference: both deliberately consented to transgress a grave commandment of God. Subjectively, however, there is a great difference. Dimmesdale "yielded himself . . . to what he knew was deadly sin." Hester had no such knowledge. "She had wandered, without rule or guidance, in a moral wilderness; as vast, as intricate and shadowy, as the untamed forest, amid the gloom of which they were now holding a colloquy that was to decide their fate. Her intellect and heart had their home, as it were, in desert places, where she roamed as freely as the wild Indian in his woods. For years past she had looked from this estranged point of view at human institutions, and whatever priests and legislators had established . . ." (V, 239). She was unaware, Hawthorne told the reader in effect, that the plan which she proposed, and to which both consented, was "a deadly sin." Dimmesdale, on the other hand, "had never gone through an experience calculated to lead him beyond the scope of generally received laws" (V, 240). He, therefore, knew that it was "a deadly sin." In the terminology of the theologians, therefore, Dimmesdale committed a formal sin. Hester committed a material sin—and a material sin brings neither guilt nor stain to the soul. In the sight of God she committed no sin at all, always assuming, of course, that her ignorance of the law was inculpable.

Hester did, however, commit a formal sin of decep-

tion. "O Arthur . . . forgive me! . . . Truth was the
one virtue which I might have held fast . . . Then I
consented to a deception. But a lie is never good, even
though death threaten on the other side!" (V, 232)

The three requisites for formal sin are clearly embodied in this confession. "I consented to a deception"
—explicit here is the admission that the act was accompanied with a full consent of the will. "But a lie is never
good . . ."—Hester asserts her full knowledge of the
evil of deception, as well as her belief that every lie is
contrary to the established order. And it is this formal
sin which she willingly confesses and for which she
realizes she must accept God's punishment.

Throughout his writings, Hawthorne remained true to
this basic distinction between formal and material sin.
Unless a man deliberately and with full knowledge of the
evil does what he thinks is wrong, there can be no question of formal sin. Aylmer, for example, had devoted
himself "unreservedly to scientific studies" to such an
extent that he sought to remove the "flaw of humanity
which Nature, in one shape or another, stamps efface-
ably on all her productions" (II, 50). He thus deliberately attempted to transgress the "natural law." But he
"aimed loftily" and wrought "nobly." In short, he lacked
a full knowledge of the evil; he strove with the best of
intentions and the highest of motives to remedy what he
considered an imperfection. He was guiltless, therefore,
of formal sin.

The sin of Reuben Bourne lay not in his leaving Roger
Malvin to die, for at the time he did so, he lacked a full
knowledge of the evil. But his failure "to disclose the
truth to Dorcas" admitted of no such extenuation. He
deliberately, albeit through "moral cowardice," deceived
her, knowing at the time that in so doing he was committing a great wrong (II, 394). Hawthorne referred
to it as a "falsehood," a "prevarication" fraught with

grave consequences for him who had practiced the deception.

Ethan Brand, too, with "cold and remorseless purpose" made Esther "the subject of a psychological experiment, and wasted, absorbed, and perhaps annihilated her soul, in the process" (III, 489). The phrase *cold and remorseless purpose* implies at once a full knowledge of the evil and a full consent of the will.

4

Such cases as those already adduced are easily soluble. Yet they are possibly the exception rather than the rule. In the normal course of events, it is most difficult for one human being accurately to read the heart of another; hence, no one can render certain judgment as to the true gravity of another's sin. By way of illustration: Hilda saw Donatello push Miriam's persecutor off the Tarpeian Rock. Now she could be reasonably certain that Donatello did not accidentally cause the model to lose his footing and tumble headlong over the parapet. But was the act she witnessed a formal sin or a material sin? How could she know whether Donatello acted with complete deliberation, with full consent of the will? Perhaps the rage of the moment weakened his will to such an extent that the deliberation requisite for a formal sin was impossible: Hawthorne seemed to indicate as much when he mentioned that the "glow of rage was still lurid on Donatello's face" moments after the deed had been accomplished (VI, 203). Perhaps, too, Miriam's look of assent infringed upon Donatello's consent, thus diminishing the voluntariness of his act and, consequently, the gravity of his sin. The dead man, Donatello told Miriam, "had his trial in that breath or two while I held him over the cliff, and his sentence in that one glance, when your eyes responded to mine!" (VI, 204)

As for a full knowledge of the evil, how could Hilda possibly judge that. The rage and passion of the moment may have so obscured his intellect that the requisite knowledge of the evil about to be perpetrated was practically nonexistent. Besides, Donatello answered Miriam's "What have you done?" with "I did what ought to be done to a traitor!" (VI, 203) If those words mean what they say, then Donatello may have felt that, far from committing a crime, he was actually about to perform a noble act.

Miriam's "sin" of consent to the "murder" presents an even greater difficulty to the casuist, for the simple reason that, if a sin at all, it was not consummated in any action for which she was physically responsible. In the minutes preceding the deed, even before the struggle between Donatello and Antonio began, "a cold sick despair crept over her . . . and benumbed her natural promptitude of thought" (VI, 202). With such a handicap, a full knowledge of the evil is readily questionable. In her subsequent recollection "of that wild moment, she beheld herself as in a dim show, and could not well distinguish what was done and suffered; no, not even whether she were really an actor and a sufferer in the scene" (VI, 202). And when Donatello told her that "your eyes bade me do" it, she could not recall that her eyes either provoked or assented to the deed. "But, alas! looking back into the frenzy and turmoil of the scene just acted, she could not deny—she was not sure whether it might be so, or no—that a wild joy had flamed up in her heart, when she beheld her persecutor in his mortal peril. Was it horror?—or ecstasy?—or both in one?" (VI, 203 f.)

Now in the face of such half-affirmations, half-denials, doubts, and contradictions, all voiced by the parties concerned with the utmost truthfulness and in the sincere desire to reconstruct their state of mind and will during the moments of the act, who is to judge the nature of the

sin committed?   Is Donatello guilty of a material or of
a formal sin?   If formal, what is its gravity?   The same
questions can be asked concerning Miriam, to be met
with the same hedging answers as in the case of Donatello.   Moral theologians, if confronted in the confessional with the accounts provided by Hawthorne in *The
Marble Faun,* would tell the penitent: "It's difficult to
assess the true nature of your guilt; confess this sin as
you are guilty in the sight of Almighty God."   For God
alone can infallibly judge motives, intentions, delibera-
tions, and knowledges.

Hawthorne follows the conversation between Miriam
and Donatello, in which they attempted to reconstruct
the details of the act, with this authorial sentence: "She
turned to him,—the guilty, blood-stained, lonely woman,
—she turned to her fellow-criminal, the youth, so lately
innocent, whom she had drawn into her doom" (VI,
204 f.).   Apparently, Hawthorne here considers Donatello and Miriam equally guilty of formal sin; indeed,
they both eventually come to look upon themselves as
criminals.   Yet they do so, I believe, in virtue of a consequent dictate of conscience.   For there is an evident
difference between an antecedent dictate of conscience,
which precedes the action, judging it to be right or
wrong, and a consequent dictate of conscience, which
follows an action, approving it as just, or condemning it
as wrong.   It is clear, too, that a consequent dictate of
conscience cannot affect the morality of an action.   This
being so, the questions concerning the nature and gravity
of the sins committed remain unresolved.

There is this to be added, however: if either Miriam
or Donatello, or both, in their protracted *post factum*
thinking, come to the objectively erroneous conclusion
that the deed committed constituted a formal sin, then
they are obligated to take the same steps toward remission as they would take had they been antecedently con-

vinced of the malice of the act about to be perpetrated. Since, in that case, they are honestly, if erroneously, convinced of their guilt, the act must be submitted to the tribunal of the confessional, if the parties are Catholics, or to whatever external or internal forum their personal beliefs dictate.

This would seem to be the spiritual condition of Miriam and Donatello. Judging from the recorded account of the act itself and from the already established pattern of Hawthorne's thinking on the nature of sin, it is highly probable that neither Miriam nor Donatello is guilty of formal deadly sin. Subsequently, however, they sincerely, though fallaciously, come to believe themselves guilty. Hawthorne adopts their point of view: subjectively they are criminals.

This somewhat intricate analysis is superfluous if one assumes that Hawthorne here loses sight of the distinction between formal and material sin, and applies the term *crime* indiscriminately to both. There is some justification for this assumption, particularly in view of his over-all purpose in *The Marble Faun*. Here, however, it need only be noted that sin in *The Marble Faun* is no longer the easily distinguishable black of *The Scarlet Letter*. There is a perceptible shading off into a zone of neutral gray, an artistic admission, as it were, that, though moral evil certainly exists, its precise nature is at times difficult to ascertain.

Hawthorne, in other words, is grappling with a problem which perturbs even the most astute anatomists of sin. That problem is this. X and Y both steal $100.00 from the neighbor next door. Both do it deliberately. X believes, erroneously, of course, that to relieve anyone of that sum is quite all right. Since he doesn't know that stealing is sinful—to be sure, his ignorance must be of the type characterized as invincible—he cannot be guilty of formal sin. Y, on the other hand, knows that what he is doing is wrong. He, therefore, commits the formal sin of theft. He incurs the guilt and stain of an actual sin. X does not.

Confronted by this illustration, one may well ask oneself, as Hawthorne must have done, "Is there, then, no objective morality? Is the individual to be permitted to set his own norms of right and wrong? Certainly it would seem so: the theological distinction between formal and material sin makes for a subjective morality."

Moralists have a traditional solution to this problem. They insist that "the fundamental norm of right conduct . . . is man's moral nature; morally right conduct is conduct in conformity with man's nature in itself and in all its relations. This constitutes right order in the moral world, which God the Creator and provident Ruler of the universe cannot but will us to observe, and this divine Will or Reason bidding us to observe right order and prohibiting its violation is the eternal law of God, the formal objective rule of morality. Human reason, applied to conduct, or conscience, is the formal subjective rule which makes known to us and applies the objective rule." [11]

This eternal law of God, then, embodying, as it does, those rules of conduct which right reason makes known to us, constitutes an objective standard of morality. This standard is an unvaryingly valid norm; in itself, it binds all men at all times. Now certain individuals or even entire tribes may be ignorant of the specific details and applications of this eternal law. In that event, such persons act contrary to this objective standard of morality in good faith, utterly without any knowledge of the inherent malice of their actions. Formal sin, therefore, cannot be imputed to them. Repeated departures from this objective norm, however, even though merely material, cause a blot on the fabric of human society and thus bring with them their own remedy.

There is, then, according to the consensus of theological opinion, an objective immutable standard of morality.

Hawthorne's exploration of the problems arising out of the distinction between formal and material sin is a continuing process. In his earliest major work, *The Scarlet Letter,* he well foresaw the dilemma to be posed by the commentators: "If Hester's right, Dimmesdale's wrong!" This quasi-epigram presumably means that if Hester's "intuitive" standards, by which she can and does justify adultery, are correct, then Dimmesdale's standards, based on the law of God, are wrong. Yet such an adolescent presentation of the problem is a vast oversimplification. Hawthorne would insist that both are wrong: Hester, materially; Dimmesdale, formally. Both transgress an objectively valid norm. Both pay, in their own way, the penalty of their sin. In Hester's case, that penalty, though inflicted perforce, is yet the occasion for a regeneration, a growth in maturity. In Dimmesdale's case—and his was a formal sin, though its gravity may have been diminished by the passion of the moment— the consequences of the sin in no way contributed to enhance the nobility of his character. Hester had no sin of adultery to repent of. Yet she was forced to pay a stern penalty for a material transgression. And in virtue of that penalty she entered upon a life of charitable service to the community. But the point is that Hawthorne, neither by authorial comment nor in the future which he as novelist assigns her, voices approval of the principle that each individual is a law unto himself.

The treatment accorded Miriam and Donatello bears out the same conclusion. The ethics of romantic individualism, the natural instincts by which each man arbitrarily decides what's right and what's wrong, are weighed in the balance and found wanting. Granting that the deed which "educated" them, the murder of the model, was not a formal sin, their life subsequent to that act can scarcely be characterized as happy. That life itself was their penalty: "a remorseful man and woman, linked by a marriage-bond of crime,—they would set forth towards an inevitable goal" (VI, 492). That goal was to be a life of penitence for Miriam, a life in prison for Donatello.

Hawthorne's belief that this objective standard of morality cannot be transgressed with impunity may be further indicated by a very general statement contained in one of his early plot outlines. He proposes to represent the "excruciating agonies which Nature inflicts on men (who break her laws) . . . as the work of human tormentors; as the gout, by screwing the toes. Thus we might find that worse than the tortures of the Spanish Inquisition are daily suffered without exciting notice." [12]

The reference, of course, may be limited to those who knowingly transgress nature's laws, though such a restriction seems unauthorized by the text. Hawthorne seems to lay it down as a principle that any infraction of the laws of nature, whether formal or material, is inevitably followed by some sort of retribution. Certainly, as an artist he exacts severe, though varying, penalties of all his transgressors, without any particular regard as to whether they violate the objective norm wittingly or unwittingly.

From the record of Hawthorne's thinking, then, there emerges this definition of sin: a deliberate and knowing transgression of an objective standard of morality. This is a general definition, which must be tailored to fit his concept either of formal or material sin. Anyone, Hawthorne would say, is guilty of formal sin if he knowingly and willingly does what he *thinks* to be wrong. If he honestly believes it is a sin to eat peas with a knife instead of a fork, and then knowingly and willingly proceeds to eat peas with a knife, that man is guilty of formal sin. Anyone, on the other hand, who performs an objectively wrong action invincibly ignorant of its true malice commits a material sin only.

It is equally clear that Hawthorne rejects the deterministic ethics of Chillingworth, the individualistic ethics of the adulteress Hester, the legalistic ethics of Judge Pyncheon. By the simple process of elimination, then, he must subscribe to an objective standard of morality known by the light of right reason, whereby man discerns what is good and what is evil.

5

Nowhere in either his journals or his tales does Hawthorne professedly treat any of the numerous problems which flow from an analysis of the nature of sin. He provides no clue by which the reader can judge whether he holds that sins are distinguished specifically by their objects, whether they differ in regard to omission and commission, or whether the gravity of the sin depends on the position of the person sinned against.

Yet it is evident that, in sharp contrast to the accepted canons of Puritan thinking,[13] he does not consider all sins as equal. In an editorial passage from "Egotism" he takes notice of the fact that all persons "chronically diseased," either in mind or body, are egotists, and that "the fouler the crime, with so much the more difficulty does the perpetrator prevent it from thrusting up its snakelike head to frighten the world; for it is . . . that crime, which constitutes their [sic] respective individuality" (II, 309). Obviously, then, Hawthorne believes one sin can be "fouler" than another. As already shown, he distinguishes between the gravity of "a sin of passion, not of principle, nor of purpose" (V, 240), and the greater gravity of a temptation yielded to "with deliberate choice" and in the full knowledge that it "was deadly sin" (V, 265). In the notebooks he records his conviction that a friend of his was guilty of "the little sin of a fretful and peevish habit . . ."[14]

The evidence proves, then, that Hawthorne believes some sins to be more grave than others. Nowhere, however, does he give any criteria whereby mortal sins can be distinguished from venial sins. Nor is there any possibility of knowing whether he holds the distinction between big and little sins to be one of degree or one of species.

There is, too, sufficient indication to show that Hawthorne considers carnal sins less grave than spiritual sins. Chillingworth's revenge was greater than Dimmesdale's or Hester's adultery. Hawthorne's concept of the "unpardonable sin" points to a conviction that sins of the mind—pride, egotism, isolation—are of greater guilt than sins of the flesh.

Whatever his reasons may have been, Hawthorne, in making this distinction, is on firm theological ground. Thomas Aquinas gives it as his opinion that carnal sin denotes a *turning to* something, "whereas spiritual sin denotes more a *turning from* something, whence the notion of guilt arises, and for this reason it involves greater guilt."[15] That Hawthorne would adopt this basis for his distinction is unlikely. He would, however, stress the fact that carnal sins "have a stronger impulse," and that the stronger the impulse, the less deliberate and, hence, the less grievous the sin.

In his fundamental concept of sin, then, Hawthorne is remarkably in agreement with the common teaching of Christianity. There are many facets of the problem of moral evil which either do not occur to him or which he chooses to ignore. Yet he does stoutly maintain that sin resides in the will—contrary to those who, theoretically, at least, denied free will and consequent moral responsibility. The will of man, Hawthorne insists, is the ultimate source of moral evil.

Not sin, but its consequences for human lives is Hawthorne's major theme.

—F. O. Matthiessen

II. THE CONSEQUENCES OF SIN

Nathaniel Hawthorne's interest in moral evil and its consequences does not make him a moralist. Nor would he have laid claim to the title. It is quite understandable, therefore, that one finds in his writings no hard and fast distinction between original sin and actual sin. Yet this distinction must precede any fruitful speculation on the consequences of sin.

According to the accepted teaching of moral theologians, original sin is that sin which everyone born into this world inherits from his first parents, namely, Adam and Eve. In virtue of this inherited sin, man comes into being with a nature corrupted, an understanding darkened, a will weakened, and a strong inclination to evil. Without intending to be facetious, one may say that the situation has been more or less adequately summed up by the wit who remarked that Adam ran the wagon of human nature into an apple tree, and that said vehicle has been in imperfect running condition ever since.

Original sin, then, is a non-personal sin transmitted to every human being, the Blessed Virgin Mary alone excepted, by the mere fact of his being a descendant ultimately of Adam. The apparent injustice of such an arrangement has engrossed the thinking of many men in every age. Their arguments and counterclaims need not concern us. Yet it is to the point of this study to consider one explanation of how the sin of our first parent could be transmitted, by way of origin, to his descendants.

"All men born of Adam," Thomas Aquinas reasons, "may be considered as one man inasmuch as they have one common nature, which they receive from their first parents. . . . Indeed, Porphyry says that 'by sharing the same species, many men are one.' Accordingly, the multitude of men born of Adam are as so many members of one body. Now the action of one member of the body, of the hand, for instance, is voluntary, not by the will of that hand, but by the will of the soul, the first mover of the members." St. Thomas then adduces in illustration of the previous step the example of a murder performed by the hand. This murder is not imputed as a sin to the hand, considered as separate from the body; rather, it is imputed to the hand as something belonging to the body "and moved by man's first moving principle." Similarly, now, "the disorder which is in this man born of Adam is voluntary, not by his will, but by the will of his first parent, who, by the movement of generation, moves all who originate from him, even as the soul's will moves all the members to their actions. . . . And just as the actual sin that is committed by a member of the body [the hand, for example] is not the sin of that member, except inasmuch as that member is a part of the man . . . so original sin is not the sin of this person, except inasmuch as this person receives his nature from his first parent . . ."[16]

Unaided human reason alone, of course, is unable to arrive at a true concept of original sin. Nor is there any record to show that Hawthorne even read, let alone understood the key passage in St. Paul's letter to the Romans: "By one man sin entered into this world and by sin death, and so death passed upon all men . . ." (5: 12). Yet the New England novelist, on more than one occasion, expressed his belief that man's human nature, antecedent to all personal sin, lacks that degree of purity one might expect from an original handiwork of God.

A rather lengthy parenthetical passage, inserted into the ninth chapter of *Fanshawe,* is one expression of such a conviction.

(It is sometimes, though less frequently, the case, that this disposition to make a " joy of grief " extends to individuals of the other sex. But in us [men] it is even less excusable and more disgusting, because it is our nature to shun the sick and afflicted; and, unless restrained by principles other than we bring into the world with us, men might follow the example of many animals in destroying the infirm of their own species. Indeed, instances of this nature might be adduced among savage nations.) XI, 201 f.

From this excerpt it is legitimate to deduce that Hawthorne believes man's inclinations, which he brings into the world with him, need restraining. This is tantamount to saying that man is born with a strong inclination to evil. Such an inclination, according to theologians, is one of the effects of original sin.

In *The House of the Seven Gables,* Phoebe is struck by the close resemblance between the living Judge Pyncheon and the portrait of his ancestor, Colonel Pyncheon. Hawthorne notes that a "deeper philosopher" than Phoebe might have drawn therefrom certain rather ominous conclusions. Speaking for himself, and presumably as the "deeper philosopher," he views this strange resemblance as an indication that "the weaknesses and defects, the bad passions, the mean tendencies, and the moral diseases which lead to crime are handed down from one generation to another, by a far surer process of transmission than human law has been able to establish in respect to the riches and honors which it seeks to entail upon posterity" (III, 147). Here again, of course, there is no specific mention of original sin, but the consequences ascribable to that sin, and its mode of transmission, are recounted with theological precision.

The notebooks contain an entry which records his belief that there is "evil in every human heart, which may remain latent, perhaps, through the whole of life; but circumstances may rouse it to activity . . ."[17] One is justified, I think, in interpreting the term *evil* in this sentence as meaning a *tendency to evil*. This tendency to evil is likewise one of the consequences of original sin.

Man, therefore, enters this world deprived of gifts which might have been his had Adam not sinned. Post-lapsarian man, then, is a deprived human being, not a depraved one; in other words, his nature is not intrinsically corrupt. Mr. Randall Stewart, I believe, is wrong in maintaining that "Hawthorne and the Puritans were in complete agreement . . . in the belief that human nature is radically sinful. In 'Fancy's Show-Box' (1837), the doctrine of universal depravity is stated with sufficient explicitness to satisfy the most rigorous theologian of the puritanical school: 'Man must not disclaim his brotherhood, even with the guiltiest, since, though his hand be clean, his heart has surely been polluted by the flitting phantoms of iniquity.' "[18]

The quotation adduced by Mr. Stewart is not too different from the Biblical "Who can say: My heart is clean, I am pure from sin?"[19] Yet the Scriptures do not teach the intrinsic corruption of human nature. To say, as Hawthorne does in effect, that all men are sinners is simply to state an orthodox and acknowledged fact. Now to determine whether they are sinners by choice or by force requires an additional statement. That statement is not forthcoming. On the contrary, Hawthorne's proved conviction that the will of man is free either to yield to or to resist temptation indicates quite clearly that he is not an adherent of the doctrine of universal depravity.

It is a justifiable conclusion, therefore, that Nathaniel Hawthorne viewed human nature as marred by "weakness and defects," by a tendency toward evil, by inclinations which need to be restrained. According to accepted theological teaching, these deficiencies are among the results of the sin transmitted to all descendants of Adam. Hawthorne, then, though he does not

treat the concept of original sin, save in so far as he has
Miriam mention the "sin . . . into which Adam precipitated himself and all his race" (VI, 491), alludes to
its consequences. Whether he specifically attributes
such consequences as those enumerated to an inherited
sin must remain uncertain. It is significant that Hawthorne was never baptized;[20] yet baptism has always
been the usual means by which man is cleansed of original sin.

2

Actual sin differs from original sin in that man himself is personally responsible for it. Hawthorne brings
the full force of his insight and perception to bear upon
his treatment of the effects of actual sin.

Sin is a stain upon the soul. That, Hawthorne would
maintain, is the logically first consequence of any sin.
"What is guilt?" he asks himself in "Fancy's Show-Box."
"A stain upon the soul." The term *guilt* here, as not in-
frequently in Hawthorne, is a synonym for *sin*. This is
sufficiently apparent from the sentence immediately succeeding: "And it is a point of vast interest whether the
soul may contract such stains, in all their depth and
flagrancy, from deeds which may have been plotted and
resolved upon, but which, physically, have never had
existence" (I, 250).

Two inferences, then, may be drawn from these statements:

1. sin causes a stain upon the soul;
2. these stains may vary in " depth and flagrancy," depend-
   ing, presumably, upon the nature of the sin committed.

Furthermore, this stain contracted by the soul as a result of sin seems ineradicable. Writing in his notebooks,
he recorded the words of a ship's captain who "observed
that he would not have had it [the violent death of a

subordinate] happen for a 'thousand dollars.' " Hawthorne objected to such a materialistic scale of values:
". . . that being the amount of detriment which he con-
ceives himself to suffer by . . . the ineffaceable blood-
stain on his hand. In my opinion, it is little short of
murder, if at all . . ." [21] He compared his bankrupt
friends to "a woman who has once lost her chastity; no
after life of virtue will take out the stain." [22] In Lord
Stanley's present character, so far as Hawthorne could
see, "there . . . [was] nothing to obliterate this early
stain" caused by stealing a five-pound note.[23]

There is an implication in this last remark that a present life more in accord with the standards of a higher
morality may somehow have obliterated Lord Stanley's
"early stain." In that event, of course, the stain wrought
upon the soul by sin can scarcely be characterized as ineffaceable. I incline to the opinion, however, that a
solemn pronouncement, purely authorial, in *The Scarlet
Letter* represents Hawthorne's final view.

And be the stern and sad truth spoken, that the breach which
guilt has once made into the human soul is never, in this
mortal state, repaired (V, 241).

One may object, it is true, to the shift in metaphor
from *stain* to *breach,* but the solemnity with which the
assertion is made justifies the contention that whatever
happens to the soul—whether *stain* or *breach*—is neither
erased nor repaired.

Properly speaking, only corporeal objects are capable
of being stained or breached. The soul, however, being
a spiritual substance, can be rightly said to suffer a loss
of splendor, a diminution of sheen, through the commission of sin. And this loss of splendor can be meta-
phorically termed a stain; in other words, the term *stain*
denotes a privation of the soul's glory in relation to its
cause, which is sin.

It is true, also, as Thomas Aquinas teaches, that this stain remains in the soul after the act of sin is past. But Thomas Aquinas denies that the stain is ineradicable: it is removed as soon as man, through repentance, returns "to the divine light and the light of reason." For that stain may be compared to "a shadow, which is the privation of light through the interposition of a body . . ."[24]

Hawthorne's analysis of this logically first consequence of sin shows a more than accidental agreement with that of the Scholastics. With them he holds that sin causes a stain on the soul, and that the stain varies according to the nature and gravity of the sin. He departs from them in so far as he seems to believe this stain to be ineffaceable.

3

In a letter to Sophia Peabody, dated September 14, 1841, Hawthorne made some suggestions which might guide her in the illustrations she was doing for *Grandfather's Chair*. "The Master," he wrote, "must be calm, rigid, without anger or pity, the very personification of that immitigable law, whereby suffering follows sin."

Here, then, is the statement of a basic principle: it is an immitigable law that suffering follows sin. And it is no exaggeration to say that his major works are an exemplification and an elucidation of this fundamental principle. By means of them, he strives to assess the nature of this suffering which is the consequence of sin.

Before one enters upon a detailed examination of this aspect of Hawthorne's thinking, it is pertinent to call attention to the fact that any author's emphasis upon a matter such as this will automatically vary with his angle of approach. Sin may be considered from what I have somewhat arbitrarily chosen to call the ontological point of view—as destructive, therefore, of the right order impressed upon the universe by its Creator. It may be studied in its sociological aspects—that is, in so far as it destroys the normal relations of men living together in society. Or it may be presented as a psychological evil —in which case the stress would be upon its repercussion on the individual who commits the sin. It is clear, of course, that any complete treatment of the consequences of sin must avail itself of all three approaches.

Nathaniel Hawthorne, while he does not, as will be shown, lose sight of either the ontological or the sociological approach, views sin primarily in its effects upon the individual, possibly on the very reasonable supposition that since it is the individual who sins, it is the individual who should pay the penalty.

Personal sin, then, stains the soul of the person sinning and, by an immitigable law, brings him suffering. Now in what precisely does this suffering consist?

The evidence proves that this suffering consists in and flows from the isolation which Hawthorne believes to be the necessary subsequent of sin. Numerous statements, explicit as well as implicit, settle this point beyond the possibility of reasonable doubt.

The general principle underlying the process by which isolation flows from wrongdoing finds adequate formulation in a purely editorial passage from "Egotism."

All persons chronically diseased are egotists, whether the disease be of the mind or body; whether it be sin, sorrow, or merely the more tolerable calamity of some endless pain, or mischief among the cords of mortal life. Such individuals are made acutely conscious of a self, by the torture in which it dwells. Self, therefore, grows to be so prominent an object with them that they cannot but present it to the face of every casual passer-by. There is a pleasure—perhaps the greatest of which the sufferer is susceptible—in displaying the wasted or ulcerated limb, or the cancer in the breast; and the fouler the crime, with so much the more difficulty does the perpetrator prevent it from thrusting up its snake-like head to frighten the world; for it is that cancer, or that crime, which constitutes their [*sic*] respective individuality (II, 309).

The principle formulated in this excerpt is broad enough to apply to both physical and moral evil. Primarily, however, it is tailored to fit the consequences of moral evil, since Roderick Elliston's physical malady is symbolic of his jealousy. The result of this sin, for Elliston, is specifically stated by Hawthorne: ". . . with a morbid repugnance . . . [Elliston] estranged himself from all companionship" (II, 307); "he drew his misery around him like a regal mantle" (II, 310). Once the knowledge of his ailment had been noised abroad, he "solicited and forced himself upon the notice of acquaintances and strangers" (II, 308). Yet despite these efforts to reestablish a kind of brotherhood between himself and his fellowmen, or perhaps because of those very efforts, he "became the pest of the city." The pest, like the plague, is carefully shunned and isolated.

There can be no doubt, then, that in "Egotism," Hawthorne registers his conviction that the suffering which follows sin is concomitant with the isolation which wrongdoing produces.

In "Roger Malvin's Burial," Reuben Bourne's sin of deception "became like a chain binding down his spirit and like a serpent gnawing into his heart; and he was transformed into a sad and downcast yet irritable man" (II, 395). His "insulated emotions . . . made him a selfish man, and he could no longer love deeply except where he saw or imagined some reflection or likeness of his own mind" (II, 396). Detailed in this characterization are the symptoms as well as the effects of isolation, an isolation which followed upon a sin of prevarication.

As for Hester Prynne, the scarlet letter, emblematic of her adultery, "had the effect of a spell, taking her out of the ordinary relations with humanity, and enclosing her in a sphere by herself" (V, 74). Usually, "wherever Hester stood, a small vacant area—a sort of magic circle —had formed itself about her, into which, though the people were elbowing one another at a little distance, none ventured, or felt disposed, to intrude. It was a forcible type of the moral solitude in which the scarlet letter enveloped its fated wearer . . ." (V, 279). "The links that united her to the rest of human kind—links of flowers, or silk, or gold, or whatever the material— had all been broken" (V, 193 f.).

Arthur Dimmesdale's sin of deception brought with it, not the physical isolation of Hester, but a spiritual estrangement far more difficult to bear. Hawthorne, speaking authorially, characterized his life as one of "unspeakable misery," a life so false as to steal "the pith and substance out of whatever realities there are around us . . . To the untrue man, the whole universe is false, —it is impalpable,—it shrinks to nothing within his grasp" (V, 177). This isolation became more palpable as a result of his deliberate consent to leave New England in company with Hester. Returning from his colloquy with her, during which the sinful decision had been reached, he encountered old Mistress Hibbens, and this encounter "did but show his sympathy and fellowship with wicked mortals, and the world of perverted spirits" (V, 265). Implicit in this remark of Hawthorne is the statement that intercourse with the ordinary everyday world is no longer open to him. Beset by a veritable barrage of what Hawthorne calls "wicked eccentricities" —among them the impulse to "teach some very wicked words to a knot of little Puritan children" (V, 263)— he "took refuge in his study," away from his fellowmen.

Roger Chillingworth's isolation is casually assumed in every chapter of *The Scarlet Letter*. He appeared "on the outskirts of the crowd" (V, 81) when Hester stood on the scaffold of the pillory at the beginning of the story. At the end, he "almost vanished from mortal sight, like an uprooted weed that lies wilting in the sun" (V, 307). Between times, "the secret poison of his malignity [infected] . . . all the air about him" (V, 231). The Puritans of the village and throughout the district shunned him as they would "Satan himself, or Satan's emissary" (V, 156).

Each of the three key personages of *The Scarlet Letter* had been guilty of sin: Dimmesdale, of adultery (a sin of passion, not of purpose), of cowardly deception, and of a deliberate yielding to what he knew to be deadly sin; Hester, of deception; Chillingworth, of diabolical revenge. And each of them, no matter what his or her evil deed was, experienced the sense of isolation, physical and spiritual, which is the inevitable consequence of sin.

In his final major novel, Hawthorne describes even more fully the estrangement which befalls Miriam and Donatello after their joint crime.

Prior to the deed, Donatello was in complete rapport with the creatures of the forest. The "green and blue lizards, who had been basking on some rock or on a fallen pillar that absorbed the warmth of the sun, scrupled not to scramble over him with their small feet"; the birds "alighted on the nearest twigs and sang their little roundelays unbroken by any chirrup of alarm; they recognized him . . . as something akin to themselves" (VI, 94). Upon his return to the ancestral seat, after the deed had been done, he attempted, on one occasion, to recapture this intimacy with his "inarticulate" friends of the forest. He failed. Instead of approaching nearer to their quondam friend, "there ensued a hurried rush and scamper of little feet"; a "venomous reptile was the only creature that had responded to the young Count's efforts to renew his intercourse with the lower orders of

nature" (VI, 287).   Donatello admitted as much.
"They know it!" he said, trembling.   "They shun me!
All nature shrinks from me, and shudders at me!   I live
in the midst of a curse, that hems me round with a circle
of fire!   No innocent thing can come near me" (VI,
288).

This isolation inflicted upon him by "the lower orders
of nature" found its counterpart in the reactions of his
fellowmen.   Hawthorne refers specifically to this en-
forced isolation in many passages of purely authorial
comment.   The deed "which Donatello wrought, and
Miriam accepted on the instant—had wreathed itself
. . . like a serpent, in inextricable links about both their
souls, and drew them into one . . . So intimate . . .
was the union, that it seemed as if their new sympathy
annihilated all other ties, and that they were released
from the chain of humanity; a new sphere, a special law,
had been created for them alone.   The world could not
come near them; they were safe!" (VI, 205)   Voices
which had long sounded familiar to them now rang with
a strange note, coming to them, "as it were, out of the
depths of space; so remote was all that pertained to the
past life of these guilty ones, in the moral seclusion that
had suddenly extended itself around them" (VI, 206).
Between them and all brotherhood or sisterhood now lay
an "immeasurable waste" (VI, 206).

This estrangement is evident even in Donatello's relations with Kenyon, who is the third remove from the
crime committed by the Count and Miriam.

"I have a weakness which I fear I cannot overcome," re-
plied the Count, turning away his face.   "It troubles me to
be looked at steadfastly."

"I have observed it since we have been sitting here . . ."
rejoined the sculptor. . . . . . "It need be no hindrance to
my taking your bust . . ."

"You may take me if you have the power," said Donatello; but, even as he spoke, he turned away his face; "and if you can see what makes me shrink from you, you are welcome to put it in the bust. It is not my will, but my necessity, to avoid men's eyes . . ." (VI, 263 f.).

Both editorially, in his own right, and artistically, through the words and actions of his character, Hawthorne stresses the isolation which encompassed Miriam. In her case, of course, this isolation was already a factor prior to the murder of the model. For though the nature of her guilt in relation to the Capuchin is very obscure, there can be no doubt that this sin, whatever it may have been, insulated her from the life-giving currents moving on all sides of her. With specific references to Miriam's position prior to the deed in which she and Donatello collaborated, Hawthorne sets down this general principle: ". . . it is one of the chief earthly incommodities . . . of a great crime, that it makes the actor . . . an alien in the world, by interposing a wholly unsympathetic medium betwixt himself and those whom he yearns to meet" (VI, 114). The same concept is phrased in a slightly varying form some pages later. "This perception of an infinite, shivering solitude, amid which we cannot come close enough to human beings to be warmed by them, is one of the most forlorn results of any . . . crime . . . that puts an individual ajar with the world. Very often, as in Miriam's case, there is an insatiable instinct that demands friendship, love, and intimate communion, but is forced to pine in empty forms; a hunger of the heart, which finds only shadows to feed upon" (VI, 138 f.).

After the murder of the model, this remoteness was intensified, perhaps because this second sin had been accompanied by a greater deliberation and knowledge of the evil than her previous sin. The heightened character of her isolation is sharply portrayed in the change in her relations with Hilda.

Hilda was standing in the middle of the room. When her friend [Miriam] made a step or two from the door, she [Hilda] put forth her hands with an involuntary repellent gesture, so expressive, that Miriam at once felt a great chasm opening itself between them two. They might gaze at one another from the opposite side, but without the possibility of ever meeting more . . . There was even a terror in the thought of their meeting again. It was as if Hilda or Miriam were dead, and could no longer hold intercourse without violating a spiritual law (VI, 241).

In "Egotism," it will be remembered, Roderick Elliston became a monomaniac; his only thought was of the serpent harbored in his breast. Constant reference to it antagonized his townsmen, caused him to be shunned as a pest. "All persons chronically diseased," Hawthorne generalized, "are egotists, whether the disease be of the mind or body" (II, 309). Miriam's fate exemplifies the validity of this law. "My mind is not active any longer," she told Kenyon, in a cold, indifferent tone. "It deals with one thought and no more. One recollection paralyzes it. . . . the certainty that I am, and must ever be, an object of horror in Donatello's sight" (VI, 323). This egotism, whatever its form, is so closely intertwined with isolation that it is difficult to determine whether it precedes, accompanies, or is consequent upon the feeling of remoteness which results from sin. Perhaps the chain of cause and effect is from sin to egotism to isolation, though the order of succession may just as logically be interpreted as proceeding from sin to isolation to egotism to greater isolation.

At any rate, it has been sufficiently demonstrated that Nathaniel Hawthorne considers this cutting off from the current of society as the primary tangible consequence of any sin. Whether this effect results only from formal sin, or from material sin as well, is somewhat doubtful, since it cannot be definitely ascertained whether Donatello's sin, for example, or Miriam's, is formal or material. I am inclined to hold that even material wrongdoing would suffice to interpose "a wholly unsympathetic medium" between the sinner and society.

In the notebooks, for example, Hawthorne jotted down his impressions of an old English lady afflicted with what might be called a tic. "Of course, it was nothing but a paralytic or nervous affliction; yet one might fancy that it had its origin in some great wrong that was perpetrated, half a life-time ago, in this old gentlewoman's presence, and either against herself or somebody whom she loved still better." [25] Now this "nervous affliction," according to the already determined pattern of Hawthorne's thinking, would lead to a certain egotism, which, in turn, would bring with it a sense of estrangement. Yet the "great wrong . . . perpetrated" was not of the woman's doing. Similarly, it appears from *The House of the Seven Gables* that even the sin of an ancestor is capable of wreaking its effect of isolation on the next generation [Clifford and Hepzibah]. It is fair to assume, therefore, that Hawthorne does not mean this estrangement to be restricted to formal sin.

4

All other effects of sin specifically noted by Hawthorne derive from and are reducible to this major form of retribution. For the guilty person—and Hester Prynne is Hawthorne's case in point—a "loss of faith [in the goodness of others] is ever one of the saddest results of sin" (V, 112). Now it is a psychological truth that those who live in worlds of their own making are wont to think themselves superior, or at least equal to the rest of mankind. Miriam and Donatello exemplify their creator's contention that the "foremost result of a broken law is ever an ecstatic sense of freedom" (VI, 207).

Again, it is quite undeniable that a man who has cut himself loose from the moorings of society by transgressing a moral standard, conformity to which is necessary for the continuance of society, should experience an initial sense of freedom.

Another immediate consequence of sin, at least of that sin committed by Donatello and Miriam, was to enroll the malefactors into "an innumerable confraternity of guilty ones, all shuddering at each other" (VI, 208). But membership in such a company is granted only to those who deny themselves, or have been denied, the companionship of moral men and women. One further result of Miriam's deed was "the deadly iteration with which she was doomed to behold the image of her crime reflected back upon her in a thousand ways, and converting the great, calm face of Nature, in the whole, and in its innumerable details, into a manifold reminiscence of that dead visage" (VI, 222). Once again, this phenomenon is but a necessary corollary of that egotism which afflicts all persons who are "chronically diseased," either "of the mind or body." This egotism in turn breeds an estrangement which is partially intentional and partially involuntary, because forced upon the egotist by one-time friends and acquaintances who now shun the man or woman thus afflicted.

The consequences of sin for the individual, then, are basically two:

1. a diminution of the soul's splendor, a concept presented by Hawthorne under the metaphor of a stain upon the soul;
2. a moral and physical estrangement from individuals and from society. At times this insulation is preceded by some form of egotism. To this isolation and egotism— comparable, it would seem, to two sides of the same coin —all other effects of which Hawthorne takes specific cognizance are ultimately reducible.

Hawthorne made it quite clear, however, that sin has its repercussions, not only upon the sinner and his equally guilty accomplices, but also upon others. These sociological effects of sin are the theme of *The House of the Seven Gables,* the moral of which is "that the wrongdoing of one generation lives into the successive ones, and, divesting itself of every temporary advantage, becomes a pure and uncontrollable mischief . . ." (III, 14). The novel, in fact, was written to "convince mankind—or, indeed, any one man—of the folly of tumbling down an avalanche of ill-gotten gold, or real estate, on the heads of an unfortunate posterity, thereby to maim and crush them, until the accumulated mass shall be scattered abroad in its original atoms" (III, 14). The adjective *ill-gotten* implies that the material riches thus transmitted to posterity were acquired through evil and sinful means. In fact, the calamities visited upon Colonel Pyncheon's descendants are ascribed by Holgrave "to the old Puritan's inordinate desire to plant and endow a family" (III, 222). Again, the adjective *inordinate* connotes a desire that is limited by no law or standard, and hence contrary to the moral order imposed upon men as creatures endowed with right reason. Hawthorne himself, in the early pages of the story, characterizes his tale as a "history of retribution for the sin of long ago" (III, 59).

Hawthorne's investigation of the manner in which this retribution works itself out upon subsequent generations led him to a twofold conclusion. In the first place, there is the possibility that each successive inheritor of the estate, "conscious of wrong, and failing to rectify it—[would] commit anew the great guilt of his ancestor, and incur all its original responsibilities" (III, 34). This mode of retribution finds illustration in Judge Pyncheon, who, having inherited an estate originally acquired through fraud and having become conscious of his false title to it, was obliged, under pain of sin, to restitute to the rightful claimants. By not doing so, he became guilty of a formal personal sin. Yet no one can deny that the grave temptation to which he thus yielded himself was not of his making or seeking. This, then, is one of the sociological effects of wrongdoing: that it provides a springboard for the sins of others.

Retribution for past sins takes also a second form in *The House of the Seven Gables*. Clifford's and Hepzibah's sufferings are the direct result of the sins of the now defunct Colonel and the still living Judge. In the case of Clifford and Hepzibah, however, the effects are primarily of a physical nature.

Actually, therefore, the romance of the Pyncheons is a treatise written to inculcate the realization that sin has its sociological repercussions both in the moral and in the physical sphere.

Hawthorne's most astute examination into the sociological effects of sin, however, is reserved for *The Marble Faun*. Particularly incisive is his study of the maid Hilda, who witnessed the crime in which Miriam and Donatello collaborated. Hawthorne again, as he so often does, prepares the way for his closer analysis by the statement of a general principle. It is, he says in effect, of "fatal decree" that "every crime is made to be the agony of many innocent persons, as well as of the single guilty one" (VI, 115). The incident which occasioned the formulation of this principle has, it is true, no relation to Hilda. It refers primarily to Miriam. Yet there is no indication that Hawthorne intends to give it only a restricted validity. Certainly his authorial comment, "Every crime destroys more Edens than our own" (*MF*, VI, 247), is corroborative proof that he is giving voice to a general truth, in this case inductively arrived at after due consideration of Hilda's altered condition.

What, then, are some of the effects upon Hilda of this sin in which she has no part? She becomes estranged from Miriam, Donatello, even Kenyon. Because she is privy to Miriam's secret, she can understand "how the sins of generations past have created an atmosphere of sin for those that follow. [This is half the burden of Hawthorne's thesis in *The House of the Seven Gables*.] While there is a single guilty person in the universe, each innocent one must feel his innocence tortured by that guilt. Your deed, Miriam, has darkened the whole sky!" (VI, 247) That torture of which Hilda speaks is increased by the growing weight of the dark secret which she alone bears, and which she feels obliged to confine within her own consciousness.

As a direct result of the crime which she had witnessed, a torpor, "heretofore unknown to her vivacious though quiet temperament, had possessed itself of . . . [her], like a half-dead serpent knotting its cold, inextricable wreaths about her limbs" (VI, 375). An awful loneliness "enveloped her whithersoever she went . . . a shadow in the sunshine of festal days! a mist between her eyes and the pictures at which she strove to look; a chill dungeon, which kept her in its gray twilight and fed her with its unwholesome air, fit only for a criminal to breathe and pine in!" (VI, 377) She, the artist, "had lost . . . the faculty of appreciating those great works of art, which heretofore had made so large a portion of her happiness." She "grew acquainted with that icy demon of weariness, who haunts great picture galleries" (VI, 382 f.).

Such consequences as those specifically enumerated by Hawthorne—torpor, loneliness, weariness—would seem particularly calculated to estrange Hilda from the companionship of her fellow-mortals. It is entirely consonant with the weight of the evidence, therefore, to maintain that the ultimate sociological effect of sin is to bring isolation upon those even who are in no way guilty of that particular sin. Certainly that is the effect of Miriam's sin on Hilda, of Colonel Pyncheon's wrong-doing on Hepzibah and Clifford, of Hester's transgression on Pearl. Both in the psychological and sociological order, therefore, the one consequence of sin which looms foremost in Hawthorne's mind is isolation, either moral or physical, and in every case of varying power and duration.

If it be asked on what basis Hawthorne builds his firm belief that "every crime destroys more Edens than its own," the answer must be sought in his antecedent conviction that no man is an island of himself. Possibly this conviction was derived empirically. Possibly, too, it may have been founded on the Scholastic dictum that all men born of Adam "may be considered as one man inasmuch as they have one common nature." But whatever its origins or backgrounds, the underlying principle finds expression in such a passage as this from *The Blithedale Romance:* "If one of us happened to give his neighbor a box on the ear, the tingle was immediately felt on the same side of everybody's head" (V, 479). In the same novel, he probes even deeper: "Our souls . . . are not our own. We convey a property in them to those with whom we associate . . ." (V, 540). And in *The Marble Faun,* Hawthorne accounts for Hilda's wretched situation—the feeling that "her own spotlessness" had been "impugned"—by saying that she "[partook of] the human nature of those who could perpetrate such deeds [as Miriam's and Donatello's]" (VI, 376).

In his investigation of the sociological effects of sin, then, Hawthorne is thoroughly logical: he formulates a general principle—whether deductively or inductively arrived at cannot be determined—and then manifests its validity in the lives of his characters.

6

If through wrongdoing the sinner inflicts upon himself the penalty of isolation, then this estrangement naturally has an effect upon the established order of society. In other words, sin cannot beget psychological effects without at the same time producing sociological repercussions. Now the penalty incurred by society because of crime presupposes the rupture of a universal order, conformity to which would result in a pre-ordained ideal. To view sin ultimately as the destruction of the moral system of the universe is to look at sin from God's point of view, to take the so-called ontological approach.

There is little evidence to warrant the assertion that Hawthorne looked at sin in this light. Sin as first of all an offense against Almighty God, as a turning away from God and a turning to creatures—this fundamental theological concept of sin he apparently did not possess, or at least did not choose to record.

His familiarity with the concept is proved, however, by the words with which Miriam phrases her rhetorical questions to Hilda: "But, have I sinned against God and man, and deeply sinned? Then be more my friend than ever, for I need you more" (VI, 242). In *The Scarlet Letter*, likewise, Hawthorne authorially refers to Dimmesdale as someone who had been, and was still, "false to God and man" (V, 235). But there is no consistent and explicit development of sin under this aspect in the writings of the New England novelist.

The guilt of man does, it is true, cause havoc in the natural order. For it is the belief of Hawthorne, expressed editorially in *The House of the Seven Gables*, that "the sympathy or magnetism among human beings . . . exists, indeed, among different classes of organized life, and vibrates from one to another. A flower, for instance, as Phoebe herself observed, always began to droop sooner in Clifford's hand, or Hepzibah's, than in her own . . . " (III, 209). In the weeks after her sin, Miriam fancied that Hilda's doves "had a look of weary expectation and disappointment,—no flights, no flutterings, no cooing murmur; something that ought to have made their day glad and bright was evidently left out of this day's history" (VI, 237). Donatello remarked to Kenyon that of late "a sort of strangeness had overgrown [the many enchanting nooks in the neighboring woods and hills] . . . like clusters of dark shrubbery, so that he hardly recognized the places which he had known and loved so well" (VI, 280). The legend of one of Donatello's progenitors Kenyon interpreted as an apologue signifying that nature's "mild influences . . . are altogether powerless in the dread fever-fit or deadly chill of guilt" (VI, 285). Even the animals, once so intimate and unafraid, now deserted the sinful Donatello (VI, 294). And in "Roger Malvin's Burial" it is recorded as fact that "a blight had apparently stricken the upper part of the oak [beneath which Roger Malvin had been left to die], and the very topmost bough was withered, sapless, and utterly dead" (II, 403).

It will have been noted, of course, that very often these deviations from the normal course of nature are recorded as part of the thought stream of persons other than the author. In view of the statement of principle contained in *The House of the Seven Gables,* however, and the consistency with which his characters believe that the aspect of nature has changed, it is legitimate to say that the one "ontological" effect of sin of which Hawthorne takes cognizance is this disturbance in the order of nature. Such an upheaval in the material realm is symptomatic of a similar upheaval in the spiritual realm.

Nathaniel Hawthorne's supposed views on the "re-
generative and educative" power of sin have been the
subject of much scholarly speculation.   Henry Arlin
Turner is representative of those who, having studied the
record of Hawthorne's thinking, declare it to be his conviction "that sin is not only the accompaniment of good,
but that it is often the cause of good, and is essential for
educating man and for subjugating his sensual nature." [26]

An examination and evaluation of the pertinent evidence warrants no such conclusion.   Admittedly, for
Hawthorne, good does at times follow evil, in a purely
chronological sequence.   The point at issue, however, is
to determine, on the basis of the record, whether sin
stands in a causal relationship to this good, or whether
sin is nothing more than the occasion for, or at most the
condition of growth, maturity, deeper insight, surer happiness.   To assume that a mere chronological sequence
of events is adequate proof of a cause-and-effect relationship is to be guilty of a serious fallacy in reasoning.

At this point, a definition of terms will facilitate the
investigation.   The meaning traditionally attached to
the term *cause* since the days of Aristotle is *anything
which has a positive influence of any sort on the being
or happening of something else*.   A *condition* is *something which must be realized or fulfilled before the event
or effect in question can happen or be produced*.   On
the side of the effect, then, there is real dependence; on
the side of the condition there is no real and positive
influence on the happening of the event.   In other words,
the influence of the condition lies in the removal of some
obstacle to the positive influence of the cause.   An ordinary example is this: windows are a *condition* for the
lighting of the room in the daytime, but the sun is the
cause.   An *occasion* is *any circumstance or combination*

of circumstances favorable to the action of a free cause.
For instance, darkness is an *occasion*, not a *cause*, not a
condition, of theft. Bad companionship is an *occasion*,
not a *cause*, not a *condition*, of sin.[27]

With these traditionally accepted distinctions clear,
it is now possible to speculate coherently on Hawthorne's
views concerning the educative value of sin.

In the notebooks, under date of June 23, 1843, he considered the possibility of penetrating "Nature's secrets."
If this could be done, "we should find that what we call
weeds are more essential to the well-being of the world
than the most precious fruit or grain. This may be
doubted, however; for there is an unmistakeable [*sic*]
analogy between these wicked weeds and the bad habits
and sinful propensities which have overrun the moral
world; and we may as well imagine that there is good in
one as in the other." [28] This notebook entry constitutes
a definite statement of belief: there is no good whatsoever in bad habits and sinful propensities. Yet if they
could in any way be the *cause* of good, this statement
could not logically have been made in its present unre-
stricted form.

It is in *The Marble Faun,* however, that Hawthorne
examines most thoroughly the relationship between sin
and the benefits that chronologically follow sin. The
subject of his investigation is Donatello primarily, and,
to a limited extent, Miriam. After his crime, Donatello
"showed a far deeper sense, and an intelligence that
began to deal with high subjects"; he evinced "a more
definite and nobler individuality." Having noted these
salutary changes in Donatello's character, Hawthorne
admits, in an undeniably authorial comment, that "sometimes, perhaps, the instruction comes without the sorrow;
and oftener the sorrow teaches no lesson that abides with
us" (VI, 302). Now if the "instruction comes without
sorrow," then clearly this sorrow, which may or may not

accompany sin, cannot be anything more than an occasion for the formation of a "nobler individuality." For A [sorrow] cannot be the cause of B [instruction] if A is ever absent when B is present.

Throughout most of the rest of his investigation, Hawthorne presents his opinions, if they be his, through the mouths of Kenyon, Miriam, and Hilda. Kenyon, for example, charts the various stages in Donatello's growth to maturity. At the first shock of his sin and misery, "there was an intolerable pain and shuddering repugnance attaching themselves to all the circumstances and surroundings of the event that so terribly affected him. . . . But as his mind roused itself,—as it rose to a higher life than he had hitherto experienced,—whatever had been true and permanent within him revived by the self-same impulse" (VI, 324 f.). But it is again clear that even Kenyon is not speaking of a causal relationship; the cause is clearly the will of Donatello himself; the shock he experienced and from which he roused himself is nothing more than a circumstance favorable to the operation of this cause.

Miriam and Kenyon discuss the same subject at length toward the end of the novel.

Miriam: "Was the crime . . . a *means* [italics mine] of education, bringing a simple and imperfect nature to a point of feeling and intelligence which it could have reached under no other discipline?"

Kenyon: "You stir up deep and perilous matter, Miriam . . ."

Miriam: "Was that very sin,—into which Adam precipitated himself and all his race,—was it the destined *means* by which, over a long pathway of toil and sorrow, we are to attain a higher, brighter, and profounder happiness, than our lost birthright gave? Will not this idea account for the permitted existence of sin, as no other theory can?"

Kenyon: "It is too dangerous, Miriam! I cannot follow you!"

Miriam: "Ask Hilda what she thinks of it . . . At least, she might conclude that sin—which man chose instead of good—has been so beneficently handled by omniscience and omnipotence, that, whereas our dark enemy sought to destroy us by it, it has really become an *instrument* most effective in the education of intellect and soul.

Hawthorne's comment: Miriam paused a little longer among these meditations, which the sculptor rightly felt to be so perilous . . . (VI, 491 f.).

No novelist, as was stated in the introductory chapter, need come to a decision between alternatives. It is permissible for him to divide his conflicting insights between his characters, in this case, Miriam and Kenyon. But Hawthorne does seem to come to a decision, in that he apparently rejects Miriam's theory by aligning himself on the side of Kenyon, who, he says, "rightly felt" these meditations to be "perilous." Naturally, one may admit that a given hypothesis is perilous, and still subscribe to it. But even were this the case, I find nothing in Miriam's statement of that hypothesis to justify the belief that sin is the cause, rather than the occasion, of good. The actual cause of his soul's growth is the man himself, cooperating with God's grace; the sin provides him with an opportunity for initiating this growth. The possession of liquor, for example, will not make a man drunk; it's only a condition of his intoxication. The cause is his drinking it.

Kenyon does question Hilda, as Miriam advised. "Is sin, then . . . like sorrow, merely an element of human education, through which we struggle to a higher and purer state than we could otherwise have attained? Did Adam fall, that we might ultimately rise to a far loftier paradise than his?" (VI, 519)

Hilda is horrified even at the thought of such a possibility; Kenyon counters by admitting that he never did believe it either. But here again, Kenyon is careful to avoid the term *cause* in his phrasing of the question. And *element* is a term so protean as to be useless in any discussion of the question.

Obviously, then, in the persons of Miriam, Kenyon, and Hilda, Hawthorne examines the transcendentalist doctrine that good arises out of evil, that evil will eventually disappear "in the ascending spiral of human development." Miriam is the proponent of this view. She is rebuffed by Kenyon and Hilda, and, I believe, by Hawthorne himself. *The House of the Seven Gables* is professedly written to prove that "the wrong-doing of one generation lives into the successive ones" (III, 14). Surely it would be folly to maintain that a life of solitude in a dungeon, the tangible result of the Faun's crime, is to be accounted a boon. Hester and Dimmesdale and Miriam cannot be said to have achieved that "higher, brighter, and profounder happiness" which Miriam envisioned. Hawthorne, then, considers the theory that sin may be the cause of good. But the recorded evidence proves that he does not adopt that theory. He is willing to admit that the sin of adultery is a *condition* for sorrow for that specific sin of adultery. But adultery cannot be the *cause* of sorrow for adultery.

Hawthorne's position is clear: sin can, in the Providence of God, be the *occasion,* not the *cause,* of good. This, as has been shown, is the point of view Miriam feels sure Hilda would adopt as her own.

. . . after all, the crime and the punishment are neither of them the most serious things in the world.

—Letter to Sophia Peabody, September 14, 1841.

III. THE REMISSION OF SIN

Nathaniel Hawthorne is far less interested in the remission of sin than in the consequences of sin. Yet the fact that he classifies certain sins as "unpardonable" (in the sense hereinafter noted) clearly indicates a conviction that there must be others which are pardonable.

The orthodox tradition of Christianity has from the very beginning incorporated into its creed a belief in "the forgiveness of sin." [29] In the light of this tradition, any sin is an offense against God. Hence, it is God who must pardon the sinner. This He does as soon as the sinner becomes reconciled to His creator by means of an act of true sorrow for the sins committed and a promise to make satisfaction for them. Included in that act of sorrow, or contrition, are a firm purpose of amendment and—for Catholics—the desire of receiving the sacrament of penance (going to confession).

Hawthorne's recorded views on the remission of sin bear only a slight and, one is inclined to say, incidental resemblance to traditional Christian doctrine. For, as has already been shown, Hawthorne alludes only obscurely to the fact that sin is an offense against God. Logically, therefore, he could not reasonably be expected to consider the remission of sin as consisting in God's pardon of the offense committed against Him. Rather, his procedure is far more complicated.

Sin, he maintains, produces suffering. This suffering takes the form of an estrangement from society as a whole, or from specific members of that society: ". . . there is no fate in this world so horrible as to have no share in either its joys or sorrows." [30] Now this estrangement brings with it—sooner or later—an inclination to be reunited with the party or parties from which the evil deed has isolated the sinner. If the guilty person submits himself to this inclination, to this desire to be restored to full communion with his fellows, then he has accomplished what Hawthorne would call the first stage in obtaining the remission of sin.

This initial turning away from self must be accompanied by repentance, or penitence, that is, by sorrow for the offense committed. In the Christian tradition, this sorrow is motivated either by the fear of hell and punishments (imperfect contrition) or by the perfect love of God (perfect contrition). Just what motivates this sorrow for sin in Hawthorne's theory of remission is a moot question. It appears, however, that this repentance, whatever its motive, should include a quasi-public admission (confession) of sin coupled with a petition for forgiveness.

This second stage, then, is generally followed by a third: satisfaction of some sort for the wrong committed. Penance—the term normally used to express satisfaction for sin—is but the outward manifestation of true inward repentance.[31]   This penance may consist either in the willing acceptance of such temporal punishments as God may see fit to visit upon the sinner or in the voluntary practice of mortification.

Nowhere in his works, of course, does Hawthorne set out in detail these stages in the remission of sin. But an examination of various pertinent passages brings to light what may reasonably be called their true equivalent.

The initial stage is more than adumbrated in the final moments of "Egotism." The sculptor, appalled at Elliston's awful affliction, asks whether there is any remedy for the loathsome evil whose outward manifestation he has witnessed.

"Yes, but an impossible one," muttered Roderick, as he lay wallowing with his face in the grass. "Could I for one moment forget myself, the serpent might not abide within

me. It is my diseased self-contemplation that has engendered
and nourished him."

" Then forget yourself, my husband," said a gentle voice
above him; " forget yourself in the idea of another! " (II,
319 f.)

Subjected to analysis, these words of Elliston show

1. a state of suffering generated by an estrangement from
   mankind. His egotism, his self-contemplation has set
   him off from his fellows.
2. a realization that the only remedy is reunion with the element from which he has become estranged.
3. an inclination toward, rather, a petition—*Could I for
   one moment forget myself . . .* —for such a restoration
   to the bosom of society.

This petition of Elliston, abetted in his case by the gentle
suggestion of his wife to forget himself in the idea of
another, is immediately followed by his plea, "Rosina!
. . . forgive! forgive!" This plea for forgiveness logically involves a confession of guilt—two constituents,
normally, of inward repentance.

There is no mention of the third stage, penance for the
sin committed, unless this be somehow implied in the
post factum acceptance of the severe punishment already
inflicted upon him, a punishment of which he was re-
lieved at the moment he petitioned for readmittance into
the society of his fellowmen. Though this is slightly
more than conjecture, the first two stages—desire for
reunion, and repentance—are clearly delineated in this
final episode of one of Hawthorne's more provocative
short tales.

The first stage along Donatello's road to recovery from
sin occurs during a somewhat lengthy conversation with
Kenyon. Donatello had thought that he might best pla-
cate Heaven by becoming a monk. The sculptor advises
against this move, saying that if he personally "were bent

upon sacrificing every earthly hope as a peace-offering towards Heaven—[he] . . . would make the wide world [his] . . . cell, and good deeds to mankind [his] . . . prayer" (VI, 308). Hawthorne, in a purely authorial comment, notes that Donatello's face "brightened beneath the stars," that "when first the idea was suggested of living for the welfare of his fellow-creatures, the original beauty [of features and expression], which sorrow had partly effaced, came back elevated and spiritualized" (VI, 309). By "living for the welfare of his fellow-creatures," Donatello would be reunited with the element from which he had become alienated; upon Kenyon's suggestion, he accepted the possibility of such a reunion, even desired it [". . . his face brightened beneath the stars . . ."]. There then followed for Donatello what Hawthorne calls "a penitential pilgrimage" (VI, 341), which led from Monte Beni to Perugia, where he stood beneath the statue of Pope Julius and "felt descending upon . . . [him] from his [the bronze pontiff's] outstretched hand" a blessing (VI, 371). The majestic figure of the Pope, "stretching out the hand of benediction over them [Donatello and Miriam], and bending down upon this guilty and repentant pair its visage of grand benignity," may well be a symbolic manifestation of the remission of their sin. They were penitent, repentant; Donatello at least had openly divulged his guilt and his repentance throughout the pilgrimage. Nor is it strange that the temporal punishment should have continued after the sin's forgiveness. In willingly accepting the civil consequences of his deed [imprisonment], he performed the necessary penance, or satisfaction, for the wrongdoing he had committed.

Hilda's return to the society from which she had become estranged follows a somewhat similar pattern. In her case, of course, there was no question of any remission of personal sin. She had merely been the unwilling witness of someone else's crime. Yet the sociological consequences of that misdeed fell in force upon her. She sought relief from these consequences by submitting herself to a priest in the confessional. In so doing, she was motivated entirely by a desire to be reunited to that society of men and women from which she had been unaccountably isolated. Her confession made, the priest "stretched out his hands . . . in the act of benediction" (VI, 412), much in the same fashion as the statue of a pontiff in the Perugian marketplace seemed to raise "his outstretched hand" in blessing upon the repentant Miriam and Donatello.

Rising from her knees, Hilda experienced, in a tangible way, her restoration to membership in the confraternity of humankind. She greeted Kenyon with warm and joyful surprise, "without shunning the glance that he fixed upon her" (VI, 415), eagerly determined to sympathize with him in any possible misfortune that might have befallen him (VI, 414).

In masterful fashion, Hawthorne indicates that Hilda is no longer an outcast, in his description of the changed reception accorded her by the doves that haunted "Hilda's tower." At her approach, these doves "flung themselves upon the air, and came floating down about her head. . . . and their joyful flutterings and airy little flights . . . seemed to show that the doves had a real sympathy with their mistress's state of mind. For peace had descended upon her like a dove" (VI, 422 f.). The evil consequences of the sin of another had gone from her; she even "returned to her customary occupations," her wanderings from gallery to gallery, "with a fresh love for them" (VI, 427).

It is important to note that in each of these three accounts Hawthorne demands some tangible sign of forgiveness: for Elliston, the words and gestures of his wife Rosina; for Miriam and Donatello, the shadowy statue of a dead Pope, apprehended at the moment with his hand apparently raised in absolution; for Hilda, the blessing of a priest in the confessional. There is no indication, however, that any one of these three—Rosina, the statue of Pope Julius, the priest in St. Peter's—is exercising a divinely-commissioned right to forgive, in the name of God, a sin against God, as is the case in the prevailing Christian teaching on confession and the remission of sin. The New England novelist, as has been said, is only obscurely conscious of sin as an offense against God, as something that estranges man from God. Rather, he views sin as an act which "dissever[s] . . . [a man] from the world," makes him "give up his place and privileges with living men" ("Wakefield," I, 162). Wakefield's selfishness, for example, renders him, in Hawthorne's own words, "the Outcast of the Universe" (I, 164). And since this is so, the forgiving party functions solely as a representative of society, welcoming the outcast back into the fold of humanity.

2

Despite a radical departure from traditional Christianity in his views on who, precisely, is juridically qualified to grant absolution to penitent sinners, Hawthorne is quite orthodox in his insistence upon repentance as an indispensable condition for the forgiveness of sin.

In his introductory chapter to *The Scarlet Letter* he refers to his witch-hunting ancestors. "I know not," he writes, "whether these ancestors of mine bethought themselves to repent, and ask pardon of Heaven for their cruelties; or whether they are now groaning under the heavy consequences of them, in another state of being" (V, 25). Unless a man repent and ask pardon of Heaven, there can be no forgiveness—such must be the interpretation of these words. Just who is qualified to give verbal utterance to the words of forgiveness is, of course, left unsaid. Had Hawthorne chosen to develop the idea, he might well have had them spoken by some now living descendant of a witch sentenced to death long ago by Judge John Hathorne; this would then be official notification that the old Judge's offspring is no longer an outcast of the universe.

In the same essay, he congratulates himself that, through his interference, "a sufficient space was allowed [certain veteran Custom House officers] . . . for repentance of the evil and corrupt practices into which" (V, 29) they had fallen.

Similarly, Governor Bellingham admonishes Dimmesdale to exhort Hester "to repentance, and to confession, as a proof and consequence thereof" (V, 88).

Repentance, then, is of the essence. Nor must repentance be confused with penance. Hester, for example, employed herself "in making coarse garments for the poor"; Hawthorne cites this fact as evidence that probably "there was an idea of penance in this mode of occupation, and that she offered up a real sacrifice of enjoyment, in devoting so many hours to such rude handiwork." Yet he judges that such "morbid meddling of conscience with an immaterial matter [resulting, namely, in her rejection, as sinful, of the joy to be derived from the exquisite productions of her needle] betokened . . . no genuine and steadfast penitence, but something doubtful, something that might be deeply wrong, beneath" (V, 107 f.). Dimmesdale, too, admits to Hester that "of penance, I have had enough! Of penitence, there has been none! Else, I should long ago have thrown off these garments of mock holiness, and have shown myself to mankind as they will see me at the judgment-seat" (V, 230). In Dimmesdale's mind, then, as in Hawthorne's, true penitence is manifested externally by a free and deliberate confession of guilt. That confession he makes

on the scaffold, in the final minutes of his earthly existence.   As for Hester, she lives out the remainder of her
life in New England.   "Here," Hawthorne informs the
reader, "had been her sin; here, her sorrow; and here
was yet to be her penitence.   She had returned . . .
and resumed,—of her own free will . . . —resumed
the symbol of which we have related so dark a tale" (V,
310).   The words *of her own free will* are significant.
A forced confession of guilt will not suffice.   Only when
it proceeds from the free will of the sinner can it be considered a manifestation of true inward repentance.

Hawthorne, then, even as the sternest moral theologian, insists upon the primacy of repentance [contrition,
penitence] as an indispensable condition for the remission of sin.   In the letter to Sophia Peabody of September 14, 1841, in which he instructs her concerning illustrations for *Grandfather's Chair,* he suggests that "the
lion's head should have a sort of sly twist of one side of
its mouth . . . in order to give the impression, that,
after all, the crime and the punishment are neither of
them the most serious things in the world."   In the sentence immediately preceding, he had referred to "that
immitigable law, whereby suffering follows sin."   The
passage is a difficult one to interpret; yet I believe that
if neither the crime nor its punishment is the most serious
thing in the world, the only element that can possibly be
more serious is the sinner's repentance of his wrongdoing.   This conjecture seems quite consonant with the
established pattern of Hawthorne's thinking on the absolute necessity of penitence.

As previously noted, Hawthorne stoutly maintains, in
an authorial passage from *The Scarlet Letter,* that "the
breach which guilt has once made into the human soul
is never, in this mortal state, repaired" (V, 241).   Similarly, in *The House of the Seven Gables,* he acknowledges
the sad truth "that no great mistake, whether acted or

endured, in our mortal sphere, is ever really set right. Time, the continual vicissitude of circumstance, and the invariable inopportunity of death, render it impossible" (III, 371).

Yet this stern insistence upon certain ineradicable effects of sin is in no way opposed to a belief in the remission of sin. Common sense clearly shows that, while I may forgive a truly repentant killer for his crime of murder, neither his repentance nor my forgiveness will restore the dead man to life. With significant variations —and for Hawthorne these would be largely sociological—the same may be affirmed of any sin. Hawthorne, then, is quite logical in maintaining at once the forgiveness of sin and the temporal continuance of certain of its consequences.

3

For Hawthorne the doctrine of the forgiveness of sin embodies these articles:

1. no sin is forgiven without true repentance, true sorrow, for the sin committed;
2. this inward sorrow manifests itself in the free confession of the guilt incurred;
3. this inward sorrow, furthermore, logically implies an admission of responsibility for the sin committed and a firm purpose not to be guilty of that sin again;
4. finally, the truly penitent sinner will experience a cessation of the primary consequence of sin, namely, alienation from his fellowmen, though not necessarily an immediate discontinuance of various punishments which may be said to constitute his satisfaction, his penance, for the offenses committed. Penance, however, is not a manifestation of penitence; the sinner may, in fact, inflict penances upon himself without being truly contrite.

There is nothing in all this, of course, to brand Hawthorne as heterodox. Viewed in the light of Christian teaching, naturally, his beliefs are vague and incomplete, a necessary consequence of his failure to consider sin as primarily an offense against an all-good God. Hence, such penitence as he demands seems to arise from purely natural motives, not from the love of God or the fear of hell; instead of being reconciled to His God, the sinner is reconciled to his fellowmen. There are indications, however, that, in the very moment the sinner ceases to be an "outcast of the universe," in that same moment, too, he becomes again a friend of God. Hepzibah, contemplating her own and Clifford's long isolation from the current of humanity, "yearned to take him [Clifford] by the hand, and go and kneel down, they two together, —both so long separate from the world, and, as she now recognized, scarcely friends with Him above,—to kneel down among the people, and be reconciled to God and man at once" (III, 203).

The story of a man, cold and hard-hearted, and acknowledging no brotherhood with mankind. At his death they might try to dig him a grave, but, at a little distance beneath the ground, strike upon a rock, as if the earth refused to receive the unnatural son into her bosom. . . . Then the body would petrify . . .

—*Passages from the American Note-Books,* IX, 24.

IV. THE UNPARDONABLE SIN

Despite its recognized importance in the total pattern of his thinking, Hawthorne's concept of the unpardonable sin has never been subjected to more than casual, hit-and-run examination. It is strange that this should be so, since Hawthorne himself seems to provide the future commentator with every necessary component of a satisfactory definition.

The Unpardonable Sin might consist in a want of love and reverence for the Human Soul; in consequence of which, the investigator pried into its dark depths, not with a hope or purpose of making it better, but from a cold philosophical curiosity,—content that it should be wicked in whatever kind or degree, and only desiring to study it out. Would not this, in other words, be the separation of the intellect from the heart? [32]

With a commendable reliance on the words of the master, Henry Arlin Turner deduces that "the unpardonable sin . . . consists of exalting the mind at the expense of the heart." [33] Professor Randall Stewart, determined to cover every possibility, is less laconic:

The exercise of such a [mesmeric] power is fundamentally wrong because it violates the sacredness of personality. Only a person utterly lacking in love and reverence for the human soul, one in whom the intellect has been overdeveloped and the emotional nature has undergone atrophy, would be capable of thus preying upon a susceptible nature. In this " separation of the intellect from the heart " and the consequent drying up of human sympathies, Hawthorne finds the unpardonable sin. [34]

Specifically he declares Chillingworth, Maule, Westervelt, Brand, and Rappaccini guilty of the unpardonable sin; they are "practitioners of the mesmeric art by which 'the sacredness of an individual is violated.'" [35]

In other words, the separation of the intellect from the heart which leads a man to violate the sanctity of the individual, that is the unpardonable sin.

Yet no sooner is this definition phrased than difficulties present themselves. Does the sin in question consist in some act which shows "a want of love and reverence for the Human Soul"? Is this act by its very nature unpardonable? Or does it consist in an attitude of mind best characterized as "the separation of the intellect from the heart"? Is this attitude of mind unpardonable? And there is yet a third possibility: must this attitude of mind proceed to an act of violation before the sinner can be held guilty of an unpardonable offense?

Clearly, these are pertinent questions. Nor is the solution an easy one. Dimmesdale, for example, admits to Hester, in his dying moments, that "we violated our reverence each for the other's soul" (V, 304). Yet neither Hawthorne nor anyone else would maintain that either Dimmesdale or Hester is guilty of the unpardonable sin.

Then there is Hollingsworth. More minutely than any other of Hawthorne's characters does he seem to approximate the unpardonable sinner. From the very beginning, Coverdale "grew drearily conscious that Hollingsworth had a closer friend [*viz.*, his philanthropic theory] than ever you could be; and this friend was the cold, spectral monster which he had himself conjured up, and on which he was wasting all the warmth of his heart, and of which, at last . . . he had grown to be the bond-slave" (*BR*, V, 382). He had surrendered himself "to an overruling purpose," becoming one of those who "have no heart, no sympathy, no reason, no conscience," prepared to "smite and slay you, and trample your dead corpse underfoot . . . if you take the first step with them, and cannot take the second, and the third, and every other step of their terribly strait path." His "god-

like benevolence ha[d] been debased into all-devouring
egotism" (V, 399 f.). "Hollingsworth's heart [was]
. . . on fire with his own purpose, but icy for all human
affection" (V, 434). To Coverdale's perception, he
"had engrossed" the hearts of Priscilla and Zenobia "into
his own huge egotism" (V, 464). Zenobia herself came
to look upon him as "a monster," a "cold, heartless, self-
beginning and self-ending piece of mechanism" (V,
566), "ready to sacrifice this girl [Priscilla], whom, if
God ever visibly showed a purpose, He put into . . .
[Hollingsworth's] charge" (V, 567). Finally, Zenobia's
suicide is of his doing: "Tell him he has murdered me!"
(V, 575)

Here, then, is a man who admittedly displayed a repeated "want of love and reverence for the Human Soul,"
who exemplifies, in so far as any man can, "the separation of the intellect from the heart." Yet is he guilty of
the unpardonable sin?

Most assuredly not. And why not? For the very simple reason that he is repentant, confesses, does penance.
Coverdale, who later seeks him out in order to learn
what fate has befallen him, notices that "the powerfully
built man showed a self-distrustful weakness, and a childlike or childish tendency to press close, and closer still,
to the side of the slender woman [Priscilla] whose arm
was within his" (V, 594). Hawthorne intends, I believe, by this description, to show Hollingsworth's desire
to be reunited to that society from which his all-devouring egotism had previously estranged him.

" I have come, Hollingsworth," said I [Coverdale], " to
view your grand edifice for the reformation of criminals. Is
it finished yet? "

" No, nor begun," answered he, without raising his eyes.
" A very small one answers all my purposes. . . ."

" Up to this moment," I inquired, " how many criminals
have you reformed? "

"Not one," said Hollingsworth, with his eyes still fixed to the ground. " Ever since we parted, I have been busy with a single murderer [namely, myself]."

Then the tears rushed into my eyes, and I forgave him . . . (V, 594 f.).

That Hollingsworth is repentant is apparent from his demeanor throughout this episode. He confesses his wrong: "I have been busy with a single murderer." Priscilla had already forgiven him; now Coverdale, a second representative of the society from which he had been alienated, forgives him too.

2

It should be abundantly clear, now, that the only way to arrive at a true understanding of the Hawthornian concept of an unpardonable sin is to examine that concept in the light of those offenses which he holds to be remissible. All the confusion and all the hedging arises from a failure to adopt this very obvious approach.

The evidence shows that adultery is pardonable (Dimmesdale and Hester). So is murder (Miriam and Donatello), wilful isolation (Wakefield), jealousy (Elliston), lack of reverence for the soul of another (Hollingsworth and Dimmesdale), deception (Reuben Bourne and Hester), even the separation of the intellect from the heart (Hollingsworth). What sin, then, is unpardonable? Undoubtedly only that sin of which the guilty party does not repent, for which forgiveness is not asked. In the proper sense of the term, therefore, the only unforgivable sin for Hawthorne must be the ultimate failure of man to ask pardon for his sins.

Here again, the New England novelist is in accord with traditional Christian teaching, which has always maintained that, in the full and proper sense of the word, there is only one sin that cannot be forgiven. That sin is the refusal to ask forgiveness, or, as it is usually called, the sin of final impenitence.

Yet this same teaching admits that the term *unforgivable sin* may be used in a derivative and improper sense, much in the same way as certain diseases are said to be *mortal,* not because they *always* bring on death, but because they are of such kind that death is *most likely* to result. Similarly, now, there are certain sins of such a nature that there is little likelihood of a man's repenting of them, though this is by no means impossible. The Scriptural text: "Amen I say to you, that all sins shall be forgiven to the sons of men, and the blasphemies wherewith they may blaspheme; but whoever blasphemes against the Holy Spirit never has forgiveness, but will be guilty of an everlasting sin," [36] is to be understood in this derivative sense. In the light of the context,[37] this declaration of Christ refers to the Scribes who deliberately attempted to undermine the Saviour's mission. Now such an attitude of mind, so long as it exists, offers no likelihood of repentance. The Lord, then, is prophesying for the Scribes a failure to ask pardon, and it is this failure to ask pardon which constitutes, properly speaking, the only unpardonable sin.

Hawthorne, too, uses the term in its secondary and derivative sense. But whereas the Sacred Scriptures use the term of any sin—such as that of the Scribes—which renders it unlikely that a man should repent and ask pardon of God, Hawthorne uses it of sins which render it unlikely that a man should repent and ask forgiveness of his fellowman. In the Christian tradition, sin estranges man from God; he must, therefore, ask pardon of God. In the Hawthornian view, sin primarily estranges man from man; he must, therefore, ask pardon of man. Now any violation of the sanctity of an individual surely betokens a state of mind in which it is highly improbable that the violator will ask for readmission into the society from which he has become alienated. So, too, anyone who, like Ethan Brand, has "ceased to partake of the universal throb," who has "lost his hold of the magnetic chain of humanity," whose "moral nature" has "ceased to keep the pace of improvement with his intellect" (III, 495)—such a one is unlikely to petition for reintegration in the society from which he has been isolated.

In one of his early notebook entries, Hawthorne included the outline for a story about "a man, cold and hard-hearted, and acknowledging no brotherhood with mankind. At his death they might try to dig him a grave, but, at a little space beneath the ground strike upon a rock, as if the earth refused to receive the unnatural son into her bosom. . . . Then the body would petrify . . ."[38] Again, such a man, who acknowledges "no brotherhood with mankind" would be very unlikely to petition for readmission to that brotherhood; he would, therefore, be guilty of Hawthorne's unpardonable sin.

Improperly, then, but nevertheless justifiably, such sins can be labeled as *unpardonable,* not because they are never pardoned [Hollingsworth obtained forgiveness], but because they are of such a nature that anyone guilty of them is highly unlikely to repent and ask to be pardoned. Not the sin of violating the sanctity of the human heart, therefore, nor pride, nor egotism, but the failure to ask forgiveness—that, for Hawthorne, as well as for Christians, is, properly speaking, the only unpardonable sin. And it is this sin of final impenitence of which Maule, Westervelt, Brand, Chillingworth, and Rappaccini are guilty.

NOTES

[1] Barriss Mills, "Hawthorne and Puritanism," *The New England Quarterly*, XXI (March, 1948), 93.

[2] St. Augustine, *De Libero Arbitrio*, III, 18.

[3] St. Augustine, *Contra Faustum*, XXII, 27.

[4] St. Thomas Aquinas, *Summa Theologica*, I-II, q. 71, a. 6, as translated in Anton C. Pegis (ed.), *Basic Writings of St. Thomas Aquinas* (New York: Random House, 1944), II, 568.

[5] Thomas Slater, S.J., *A Manual of Moral Theology* (Cincinnati: Benziger Brothers, 1918), I, 116 f.

[6] *Ibid.*, I, 57.

[7] *Passages from the American Note-Books*, IX, 35.

[8] Marion L. Kesselring, "Hawthorne's Reading, 1828-1850," *Bulletin of the New York Public Library*, LIII (March, 1949), 133.

[9] For a detailed analysis of the parallel between Taylor and Hawthorne, cf. Neal F. Doubleday, "The Theme of Hawthorne's 'Fancy's Show-Box,'" *American Literature*, X (November, 1938), 341-3.

[10] John C. Gerber, "Form and Content in *The Scarlet Letter*," *The New England Quarterly*, XVII (1944), 26.

[11] Slater, *op. cit.*, I, 42.

[12] *Passages from the American Note-Books*, IX, 89.

[13] Miller, *op. cit.*, p. 45.

[14] *The French and Italian Notebooks*, II, 271.

[15] St. Thomas Aquinas, *Summa Theologica*, I-II, q. 73, a. 5, as translated in Pegis (ed.), *op. cit.*, II, 591.

[16] St. Thomas Aquinas, *Summa Theologica*, I-II, q. 81, a. 1, as translated in Pegis (ed.), *op. cit.*, II, 666.

[17] *Passages from the American Note-Books*, IX, 43.

[18] *The American Notebooks*, p. lxxii.

[19] Prov. 20: 9. For similar statements, cf. James 3: 2; 3 Kings 8: 46; 1 John 1: 8.

[20] *The American Notebooks*, p. 189.

[21] *The English Notebooks*, p. 27.

[22] *Ibid.*, p. 605.

[23] *Ibid.*, p. 53.

[24] St. Thomas Aquinas, *Summa Theologica*, I-II, q. 86, a. 1, 2, as translated in Pegis (ed.), *op. cit.*, II, 705 ff.

[25] *The English Notebooks*, p. 463.

[26] Henry Arlin Turner, "A Study of Hawthorne's Origins" (Unpublished Ph.D. dissertation, Department of English, University of Texas, 1934), p. 169.

[27] P. Coffey, Ph.D., *Ontology* (New York: Longmans, Green and Company, 1914), pp. 357-359.

[28] *The American Notebooks*, p. 186.

[29] Article 10 of the Apostles' Creed, dating from the third century.

[30] Letter to H. W. Longfellow, June 4, 1837.

[31] For a more detailed account of this third stage, particularly as it applies to *The Scarlet Letter*, cf. Gerber, *loc. cit.*, pp. 25-55.

[32] *The American Notebooks*, p. 106.

[33] Henry Arlin Turner, "A Study of Hawthorne's Origins" (Unpublished Ph.D. dissertation, Department of English, University of Texas, 1934), p. 28.

[34] *The American Notebooks*, p. lxxvi.

[35] F. O. Matthiessen departs from the key authorial passage of the notebooks. He believes that the unpardonable sin may be an "egotism that mistakes its own will for the promptings of God." Cf. F. O. Matthiessen, *American Renaissance* (New York: Oxford University Press, 1941), p. 653.

[36] Mark 3: 28, 29.

[37] For a more complete discussion of the immediate context of the passage, cf. Fr. James, O.F.M. Cap., "The Philosopher's Stone," *The Catholic Voice* (March, 1949), pp. 410-412.

[38] *Passages from the American Note-Books*, IX, 24.

I would say, ' He is a sinner,—
Never goes inside a chapel,
Only sees outsides of chapels,
Says his prayers without a chapel! '

—Henry Bright: " Song of Consul Hawthorne " [1]

[1] Quoted in Moncure D. Conway, *Life of Nathaniel Hawthorne* (London: Walter Scott [n.d.]), p. 193.

Religion

During the half-century preceding the birth of Hawthorne, the prevailing Protestantism of New England was in a condition which can best be described as one of extreme fluidity and flexibility.

Even prior to 1750, Puritanism had been subjected to varying stresses and strains; in fact, the history of that episode in the Protestant movement known as New England Puritanism is largely one of charting the dogmatic deviations and reconciliations within the ranks of its clergy and laity. Basically, these internal difficulties had their origin in the ever recurring attempts made to bridge the chasm existing between the hard and fast Calvinistic ideology, to which Puritanism paid a staunch verbal allegiance, and the growing necessity to depart, in practice, from the demands of this ideology. Cultural and economic forces at work in the eighteenth century, the growing spirit of democratic independence, which, though primarily political, had its repercussions in matters of religion—these factors, coupled with a pronounced tendency to subject the various contradictory assumptions of Calvinistic Puritanism to analysis and examination, abetted the gradual change from piety to moralism and thus deprived the pristine Puritan orthodoxy of its essential unity and coherence. Stop-gap measures, such as the so-called Half-Way Covenant of 1657-62, afforded a temporary stay of dissolution; yet in so far as it tacitly admitted the possibility of man's saving himself, this covenant denied the basic dogmatic tenet of Puritanism, the arbitrary sovereignty of God.

During the century after the adoption of the Half-Way Covenant, which was nothing less than a theological compromise designed to maintain a church which, theoretically, should consist only of regenerated members, the internal quarrels grew in violence. The rigoristic element insisted upon its view that conversion—and religion—was exclusively "an inner assurance of election." The Arminian element affirmed, with equal violence, that religion was a sober decision on the part of man to trust in God and obey His law; in other words, man could contribute to his own salvation: God was constrained by a self-imposed code of equity to grant heaven to those who live good moral lives. A plethora of distinctions, affirmations, counter-affirmations, and compromises diluted the marrow of orthodox Puritanism to such an extent that even Chauncy's Universalism—the final deification of God's benevolence—found a ready acceptance. Piety was dead. Moralism was moribund. No matter what man did, in the last analysis he could not escape salvation.

It is important to remember, however, that this radical transmutation of doctrine occurred within the accepted framework of Puritanism; that is to say, Chauncy considered himself as much a minister of the Puritan religion as Edwards or, at a later date, Hopkins. Theoretically, he may have been a heretic. But he was no schismatic. Sooner or later, however, the line of demarcation between Puritan and Arminian had to be drawn. When that time came, the separation into denominations became mandatory. Such a separation, of course, demanded a long period of incubation: Jonathan Mayhew, minister of Boston's First Church from 1747 to 1766, is generally conceded to have been New England's first outspoken Unitarian. He rejected the Calvinistic doctrines of man's total depravity and a triune God; he insisted upon reason as the final court of appeal. William Bentley and Charles Chauncy espoused doctrines substantially in conformity with those preached by Mayhew. Between 1815 and 1825, this liberal element in Puritanism was forced to declare its open and irreconcilable opposition to the conservatives and to announce the official formation of a new denomination, the Unitarian. Ten years later, the liberals among the Unitarians in turn estranged themselves from the parent sect and became known as transcendentalists.[1]

The religious milieu, then, into which Hawthorne was born and in which he spent most of his life was not one particularly designed to inculcate the acceptance of immutable dogmas. On all sides of him, chronologically as well as spatially, doctrines which had become part of the very character of New England were being put aside as no longer tenable; and no sooner had these been discarded than their substitutes were rejected with equal abandon.

Confronted and beset by this almost unparalleled elasticity in the supposedly eternal verities, Nathaniel Hawthorne may well have taken a skeptical view of all this intra- and extra-denominational strife, as well as of the sects that derived their existence through such means. In fact, it is highly probable that his consistent refusal actively to affiliate himself with any sect or any church is directly attributable to the pervading unfavorable impression made upon him by the doctrinal flexibility of his age. Like the ice on the rivers of spring, the old beliefs were breaking up; there was no point in jumping out upon an unstable, constantly moving element. Better to stay on shore. Better not to become involved.

2

The violent denominational upheavals of the early nineteenth century did not undermine the beliefs of all New Englanders. Mrs. Elizabeth Hawthorne, the novelist's mother, continued "a minute observer of religious festivals, fasts, feasts, and Sabbath days."[2] There are indications that she attempted to persuade her son to study for the ministry. Hawthorne, however, rejected her suggestion: in a letter dated March 7, 1820, he told her bluntly, "A Minister I will not be." Yet she must have renewed her efforts in that direction, for a year later, under date of March 13, 1821, he again expressed his disapproval, this time in stronger terms.

The being a Minister is of course out of the Question. I should not think that even you could desire one to chose [sic] so dull a way of life. Oh no Mother, I was not born to vegetate forever in one place, and to live and die as calm and tranquil as—a Puddle of Water.

Strangely enough, there are few indications in his writings of even the normal New Englander's interest in religion during the early years and the decade after 1821.[3] "No evidence exists of any of those religious doubts and philosophical questionings which seem so essential a part of adolescence,"[4] and which Hawthorne must have felt during his years at Bowdoin. He freely admitted being "sometimes afflicted with the Sunday Sickness,"[5] and the bill paid by him on June 22, 1822, for the term ending May 8, 1822, included a 40¢ fine for absence from public worship and a 20¢ fine for absence from Sunday recitation.[6] When one considers that his tuition and rent for that same period amounted to only $11.00, these fines are rather sizable. His life-long friend, Horatio Bridge, remembered that "mathematics and metaphysics, as studies, he disliked and neglected, to his frequent discredit in the recitation-room."[7] But facts such as these constitute only the outer shell of his Bowdoin life. They should not be overstressed.

Nor do the holdings of the various libraries to which he had access during those years provide an adequate index to the trend of his thinking. The catalog of books (approximately 800 volumes) in the library of the Athenaean Society of Bowdoin College shows very few religious works. These few include, however, a *Compendium of the Bible, Christ is Precious, Catachetical [sic] Compend[ium], Doctrine of Universal Restoration Refuted, Defense of Christianity*.[8] Whether Hawthorne himself ever consulted these volumes has not been ascertained; it is of record, however, that he was a member of the Athenaean Society of Bowdoin and in that capacity assisted in donating some of the books to its library.

Marion L. Kesselring's study, "Hawthorne's Reading, 1828-1850," based on the Salem Athenaeum's "charge-books," proves that of all the books charged out under Hawthorne's name during the years 1828 to 1850, only 10% were of a religious and/or philosophical nature,[9] and only 3½% of an undeniably religious character.[10] Again, there is no evidence that he read all the books charged out to him, or even saw them; it can be demonstrated, for example, that at one time during this period he was in Boston (as editor of *The American Magazine of Useful and Entertaining Knowledge*), and at other times off on his travels. In a letter to Longfellow, dated June 4, 1837, he admitted his very casual approach to the wisdom of the printed page.

You give me more credit than I deserve, in supposing that I have led a studious life. I have, indeed, turned over a good many books, but in so desultory a way that it cannot be called study, nor has it left me the fruits of study.

Nor is it to be assumed that Nathaniel Hawthorne compensated for his comparatively infrequent and casual reading of religious works by an exaggerated attempt to steer those conversations in which he participated into theological channels. By temperament shy and retiring, he was not the man to assume the initiative in determining the trend of conversation. Entries in his notebooks do, however, indicate one or the other widely spaced occasion when the conversation did assume a religious turn. During his visit to Bridge at Augusta, Maine, in 1837, Monsieur Schaeffer and Bridge and Hawthorne sat "in the twilight, or after Bridge . . . [was] abed, talking of Christianity and Deism [Schaeffer was a deist], of ways of life, or marriage, of benevolence,—in short all deep matters of this world and the next." [11] A year later, he talked "with one man about whether it would be worth while to grow young again, and the duty of being contented with old age;—about predestination and free-will, and other metaphysics." [12] The journals of the early 1850's mention long conversations with Herman Melville. An entry of August 1, 1851, reads: ". . . I put Julian to bed; and Melville and I had a talk about time and eternity, things of this world and of the next, and books, and publishers, and all possible and impossible matters, that lasted pretty deep into the night." [13] Again, during their stay in England, the Hawthornes had Melville as a house-guest for a three-day period. "Melville, as he always does, began to reason of Providence and futurity, and of everything that lies beyond human ken . . ." [14]

Conversations such as these, however, were not the inevitable lot of those who made the acquaintance of the New England novelist. Richard Henry Stoddard, for example, remembered having had dinner with Hawthorne in the summer of 1852. "We chatted, I have forgotten about what, but certainly not 'of fate, free-will, foreknowledge absolute,' but most likely about books and men." [15]

On the basis of the record, therefore, Hawthorne entertained no extensive doubts about his status as a New Englander unaffiliated with any religious denomination. There was a time, it is true, shortly after his graduation from Bowdoin, when he gave some thought to joining the Shakers. Under date of August 17, 1831, he wrote to his sister Louisa: "On the whole, they lead a good and comfortable life, and if it were not for their ridiculous ceremonies, a man could not do a wiser thing than join them. . . . I spoke to them about becoming a member of the Society, but have come to no decision on that point." On September 9, 1831, he referred to the same possibility in a letter to his cousin John Dike: "I have some idea of joining the Shakers, as I had an opportunity of inspecting one of their villages . . . and was much pleased with their manner of life." Two months later, on November 4, 1831, he reminded his sister, Louisa, in a half-humorous vein, ". . . when I join the Shakers, I will send . . . a great slice of rye-and-indian bread." In "The Canterbury Pilgrims" (III, 518-530) the Shakers are portrayed as the symbol of a noble but impossible ideal.

His high regard for this religious sect, however, eventually spent itself. Accompanied by young Julian, he had occasion to revisit one of their villages, only to discover "that all their miserable pretence of cleanliness and neatness is the thinnest superficiality"; "the Shakers are and must needs be a filthy set." Their lack of privacy and the systematic supervision of one man over another particularly galled him; "the sooner the sect is extinct the better—a consummation which, I am happy to hear, is thought to be not a great many years distant." He excoriated them as "the most singular and bedevilled set of people that ever existed in a civilized land," even going so far as to record that when Julian "desired to comfort [?] himself," he was not at all "unwilling that he

[Julian] should bestow some [at this point a line is missing] . . . the system and establishment of these foolish Shakers." [16]

Why Hawthorne should have found himself attracted to the Shakers must remain a matter for conjecture. It is possible, of course, that the unanimity with which this sect was reviled, a unanimity by means of which the various strands of Puritanism resolved themselves into a dubious negative unity, may have aroused his interest and forced a tentative investigation. Be that as it may, the recorded evidence shows that he never again seriously conceived the notion of affiliating himself with any institutionalized form of religion.

3

In "The Celestial Railroad" Nathaniel Hawthorne rejected transcendentalism as a possible golden mean between Roman Catholicism and paganism. Into the cavern at the valley's end, where once dwelt "two cruel giants, Pope and Pagan," a single "terrible giant has [now] thrust himself," seizing "upon honest travellers and fatten[ing] them for his table with plentiful meals of smoke, mist, moonshine, raw potatoes, and sawdust." Furthermore, it is the "chief peculiarity of this huge miscreant [called Giant Transcendentalist] that neither he for himself, nor anybody for him, has ever been able to describe them [his form, his features, his substance]"; he looks "somewhat like an ill-proportioned figure, but considerably more like a heap of fog and duskiness"; and he shouted after the passersby "in so strange a phraseology that we knew not what he meant, nor whether to be encouraged or affrighted" (II, 224).

That this caricature represents Hawthorne's true appraisal of transcendentalism is clear, not only from the very nature of "The Celestial Railroad" and the Reverend R. C. Waterston's reaction to it,[17] but also from various non-fictional comments, directed for the most part at Ralph Waldo Emerson. Ellery Channing, for example, is described as "one of those queer and clever young men whom Mr. Emerson (that everlasting rejecter of all that is, and seeker for he knows not what) is continually picking up by way of a genius. There is nothing very peculiar about him." [18] Previously, he had decided that it "would be amusing to draw a parallel between him [Edmund Hosmer] and his admirer, Mr. Emerson—the mystic, stretching his hand out of cloudland, in vain search for something real . . . Mr. Emerson is a great searcher for facts; but they seem to melt away and become unsubstantial in his grasp." [19]

The half-humorous recounting of the arrival of Miss Margaret Fuller's fractious "transcendental heifer" at Brook Farm,[20] and the rebellion of the herd "against the usurpation of Miss Fuller's cow" [21] is further indication of his lack of respect for the attitude of life known as transcendental. As for Henry Thoreau, he "is somewhat tinctured with Transcendentalism; but I think him capable of becoming a very valuable contributor to your Magazine." [22]

Hawthorne rejected transcendentalism, then, because he considered it vague, impractical, tinged with too much of the mystical.

For related reasons, he found it difficult to accept Episcopalianism. On October 30, 1853, he attended the Cathedral service at Chester, England, and listened to "a little meagre discourse, which would not at all have past muster among the elaborate intellectual efforts of New England ministers." [23] Easter Sunday, April 12, 1857, found him present at an Anglican service in London. "The spirit of my Puritan ancestors," he later wrote in his journal, "was mighty in me, and I did not wonder at their being out of patience with all the mummery, which seemed to me worse than papistry because it was a corruption of it." As for the sermon on that occasion, it could only be characterized as "the coldest, dryest, most superficial rubbish." This, he noted, was in sharp contrast to the Puritans, who "showed their strength of mind and heart by preferring a sermon . . . into which the preacher put his whole soul and spirit . . . lopping away all these externals, into which religious life had first gushed and flowered, and then petrified." [24]

His opinion of the authorized representatives of so-called modern religious sects was equally unfavorable. In examining Dr. Ripley's library, he discovered "volumes of the Christian Examiner and Liberal Preacher, modern sermons, the controversial works of Unitarian ministers, and all such trash," all of which pointed up "the difference between the cold, lifeless, vaguely liberal clergyman of our own day, and the narrow but earnest cushion-thumper of puritanical times. On the whole, I prefer the last-mentioned variety of the black-coated tribe." [25] "I find my respect for clerical people, as such, and my faith in the utility of their office, decreases daily. We certainly do need a new revelation—a new system—for there seems to be no life in the old one." [26] "Protestantism needs a new Apostle to convert it into something positive." [27]

Fundamentally, his strictures against transcendentalism, Unitarianism, Episcopalianism, and their varying by-products are all reducible to one serious defect: they are vague, cold, formal, lacking the warmth and, above all, the positive character which Hawthorne considered the touchstones of a satisfying religion. The results were only too apparent: Englishmen, he wrote, "bring themselves no nearer to God when they pray, than when they play at cards." [28] Their typical clergymen pray "with great propriety of manner, but no earnestness." [29] The afternoon-service at St. Paul's in London seemed long drawn out to him: "after all, the rites are lifeless in our day." [30]

In the accepted sense of the term, therefore, Nathaniel Hawthorne was not a religious man. He attended church only by way of exception,[31] was unalterably opposed to all attempts at proselytizing,[32] and cannot in any sense be considered a sectarian. His non-sectarian status is explicitly noted in a letter written by Louisa Hawthorne to her sister-in-law, on March 4, 1843: "I do not know of any news to write you [;] people have been going to meeting all winter, and we hear of little else, but that is not in *your* line you being *beyond* the Church, as Mr [.] Parker says."

Purely subjective reasons may, of course, have been sufficient to keep him free of all denominational ties, though this seems somewhat unlikely in view of his intensely religious temperament. It seems more probable, therefore, that the proximate cause may well be found in the objective insufficiency of the various sects with which he was familiar. That this hypothesis demands careful consideration should be evident from even a casual glance at the books which appeared in 1836, the year Hawthorne went to Boston to become editor of *The American Magazine of Useful and Entertaining Knowledge*. In that year appeared Emerson's *Nature,* Orestes Brownson's *New Views* (ca. 1836), Convers Francis's *Christianity as a Purely Internal Principle,* Alcott's *Conversations with Children on the Gospels,* Ripley's *Discourses on the Philosophy of Religion,* W. H. Furness's *Remarks on the Four Gospels.* Significantly, everyone of these publications openly censured the prevailing Unitarianism for its icy respectability, its dearth of emotion. Emerson found a haven in transcendentalism. Brownson achieved a preliminary synthesis of Protestantism and Catholicism, which later led him into the Church of

Rome. Hawthorne, unable to accept the "cloud-land" of transcendentalism, reluctant to embrace the "dismal severity of the Puritanic code of law" (*SL*, V, 72), unimpressed by Brownson's "extravagant assertiveness . . . and his acceptance of many theories in rapid succession," [33] simply remained aloof. For him there was no place to go.

4

In the winter of 1858, Hawthorne, with his family, arrived in Italy. When he returned to England the summer of the following year, he returned a captive, by his own admision. Now "that I have known it once, Rome certainly does draw into itself my heart, as I think even London or even little Concord itself, or old sleepy Salem, never did and never will." [34] Not a place, he wrote, which "took so strong a hold of my being, as Rome, nor ever seemed so close to me, and so strangely familiar . . . though I have been very miserable there . . . still I cannot say I hate it—perhaps might fairly own a love for it." [35]

The Rome which Hawthorne grew to know and love was inseparable from the Eternal City, the seat of Christendom, the See City of Roman Catholicism. On all sides of him he saw unimpeachable evidence of a Church ever old, ever new. At every turn he found the living record of an institution that had survived for eighteen hundred years in a world all too prone, as he well knew, to change its beliefs with alarming regularity. Partial as he was to the architectural glories of antiquity and to the conservatives "who still, in [the] . . . intangibility and mistiness of affairs, kept a death-grip on one or two ideas which had not come into vogue since yesterday morning" (*BR*, V, 480), it is not surprising that both *The Marble Faun* and *The French and Italian Notebooks*

should be well seasoned with accounts of his reactions
to this most ancient form of Christianity.

The New England novelist found much to admire in
Roman Catholicism. Deficiencies to which he had objected in the various forms of Protestantism had been
remedied in this religion whose outward manifestations
he could not escape.

He was impressed, as any tourist would be, by the
hospitality of Catholic Italy, an aspect that struck him
most forcefully only after his departure. At Geneva he
made an unsuccessful attempt to see the inside of the
city's churches: "This being a protestant country, the
doors were all shut, an inhospitality that made half a
Catholic of me." [36]

In this center of Catholicism, too, he found little of
the emotional thinness and cool formality of transcendentalism, Unitarianism, and even Anglicanism. Pictures and paintings commemorative of the Saviour's passion and death, or the life of some saint, looked down
upon him from every altar, from the sides of every tran-
sept. Occasionally, as he became "sensible of a certain
degree of emotion in looking at an old picture . . . of
Christ bearing the cross . . . a sense of his agony . . .
came knocking at my heart, and partly got entrance."
And at such times, he thought it "a pity that Protestantism should have entirely laid aside this mode of appeal-
ing to the religious sentiment." [37]

But the Catholic churches of Rome were more than
ecclesiastical art galleries. They offered "a cool, quiet,
silent, beautiful place of worship in even the hottest and
most bustling street." Those who enter leave "the fret
and trouble of the world at the threshold"; they purify
"themselves with a touch of holy water" and kneel down
"to hold communion with some saint, their awful friend;
or perhaps confessing all their sins to a priest, laying the
whole dark burthen at the foot of the cross, and coming

forth in the freshness and elasticity of innocence." [38]
Such "inestimable advantages" Hawthorne was quick to
note with approval, regretting at the same time their
absence in Protestantism. [39]

The more Hawthorne saw of the Catholic Church, the
more he wondered "at the exuberance with which it responds to the demands of human infirmity." [40]   Nor is
it surprising that the one element which should have impressed him above all others in this "exuberance" was
the practice of going to confession.   More than anything
else in the Church, the confessor-penitent relationship
filled a long-felt need, provided a solution to the problems confronting a man who had spent a lifetime thinking about sin.   His notebooks contain a minute description of the confessional: "a little oaken structure about
as big as a century [sentry]—box, with a closed part for
the priest to sit in, and on open one for the penitent to
kneel in, and speak through the open work in the priest's
closet." [41]   More than once he stood about, "curious to
see how long it would take her [a woman penitent] to tell
her sins, the growth of a week or two, perhaps."   Though
the penitent under observation had already started her
confession when Hawthorne began his vigil, "nearly an
hour passed, before the priest came suddenly out of the
confessional, looking weary and moist with perspiration."
The next day he "watched another woman, and she, too,
was very long about it . . . When her confession was
over, the woman came and sat down on the same bench
with me, where her broad-brimmed straw-hat was lying.
She seemed to be a country-woman, with a simple, ma-
tronly face, which was solemnised and softened with the
comfort that she had got by disburthening herself of the
soil of worldly frailties, and receiving absolution." [42]

As for the confessor, Hawthorne was certain that it
"must be very tedious to listen, day after day, to the
minute and common-place iniquities of the multitude of

penitents; and it cannot be often that these are re-deemed by the treasure-trove of a great sin."[43] Yet he felt equally sure that the "relation between the confessor and his penitent might and ought to be, one of great tenderness and beauty."[44]

Especially was he impressed by the many opportunities which the Catholic Church afforded her adherents to avail themselves of the consolations of confession. In one of the transepts of St. Peter's he found "a range of confessionals, where the penitent might tell his sins in the tongue of his own country, whether French, German, Polish, English, or what not." Reminiscent of Hilda in *The Marble Faun* is his admission: "If I had had a murder on my conscience or any other great sin, I think I should have been inclined to kneel down there, and pour it into the safe secrecy of the confessional." So convinced was he of its value that he could not refrain from exclaiming: "What an institution that [the confessional] is! Man needs it so, and it seems as if God must have ordained it. This popish religion certainly does apply itself more closely and comfortably to human occasions, and I cannot but think that a great many people find their spiritual advantage in it, who would find none at all in our formless mode of worship!"[45]

Instinctively he saw another glaring contrast between Catholicism and Protestantism. In the church of San Paulo, he watched "a young man standing before a shrine writhing and wringing his hands in an agony of grief and contrition." How fortunate, he thought, this young man was; had he "been a protestant . . . he would have shut all that up within his heart, and let it burn there till it seared him."[46]

In the Catholic religion, then, Hawthorne, discovered many admirable features: its hospitality and informality,[47] its high regard for the emotional demands of human nature, above all, its very satisfying relationship of confessor and penitent. One cannot, he wrote, "think it is all a farce when you see peasant, citizen, and soldier, coming into the church, each on his own hook, and kneeling for moments or for hours, directing his silent devotions to some particular shrine; too humble to approach his God directly, and therefore asking the mediation of some saint who stands beside His infinite presence." [48]

5

Yet these qualities were offset by others which aroused his hearty disapproval. Aesthetic repulsion counteracted aesthetic attraction. In the midst of great sublimity and beauty, he found evidence of almost unbelievable tawdriness. The Italians "spit on the glorious pavement of St. Peter's and wherever else they like; they place mean-looking confessionals beneath its sublime arches, and ornament them with with [sic] cheap little colored prints of the crucifixion; they hang tin hearts and other tinsel and trumpery at the gorgeous shrines of the saints, in chapels that are encrusted with gems, or marble almost as precious; they put pasteboard statues of Saints beneath the dome of the Pantheon; in short they let the sublime and the ridiculous come close together, and are not in the least troubled by the proximity." [49]   But Hawthorne himself was troubled, as any man would be who looked upon table manners as moral precepts.[50]   Even "the old heathen deities," he was sure, "were [n]ever cheated with similar sham jewellery [sic]" as the tin-hearts now hanging at the shrines of the saints in the Pantheon.[51]

More telling than his aesthetic repugnance was a conviction that the morals of Catholics belied their dogmas, that there was an unbridgeable chasm betwen belief and practice. Both among clergy and laity he found evidences of this dichotomy. Already in 1836, he had told the readers of *The American Magazine of Useful and Entertaining Knowledge* (issue of March, 1836) that "the monks of the Greek Church were accustomed to contend with those of the Church of Rome, for the privilege of celebrating Mass in the Holy Sepulchre; and it is a curious and rather melancholy fact, that these Christians have shed blood in such a quarrel, in that place of awful sanctity—and the unbelieving Turks have interfered to keep the peace!"[52] His approval of "the exuberance with which it [the Catholic Church] responds to the demands of human infirmity" was tempered by a restriction: "If its ministers were themselves a little more than human, they might fulfill their office, and supply all that men need."[53] In a later entry he wrote, "I heartily wish the priests were better men, and that human nature, divinely influenced, could be depended upon for a constant supply and succession of good and pure men, their religion has so many admirable points."[54]

As for the laity, Hawthorne was actually surprised "that the Catholics . . . [were] not better men and women." Were it possible to "see any good effects in their daily life, we might deem it an excellent thing to be able to find incense and a prayer always ascending, to which every individual may join his own."[55] The attendants in churches seemed "quite as venal as most other Italians";[56] servants would steal oil in order to be able to burn a lamp before a statue of the Blessed Virgin Mary;[57] and he was sure that "Catholic and Italian morality would think a false oath even on the crucifix a venial crime, the object being to secure the welfare of an orphan child."[58]

This failure of priests and people to meet the high and somewhat arbitrary standards of morality set for them by Hawthorne's New England conscience might perhaps best be explained by the supposition that Catholicism as it existed in the mid-nineteenth century was but a watered-down form of an ancient and more glorious Christianity. So, at least, Hawthorne may have conjectured, for he constantly kept reminding himself of the adulterated character of the Roman Church. He was willing to admit, for example, that "Catholic religious institutions, although greatly perverted from the pristine purity of their origin, accomplished a vast deal of good, during the dark and bloody centuries in which they flourished." [59] The frescos in the interior of Italy's churches, once brilliant, now partially obliterated, were to him "the symbol of the living spirit that made Catholicism a true religion, and glorified it so long as it did live; now, the glory and beauty have departed from one and the other." [60] "In however adulterated a guise, the Catholics do get a draught of devotion to slake the thirst of their souls, and methinks it must needs do them good, even if not quite so pure as if it came from better cisterns, or from the original fountain head." [61]

Yet, no matter how diluted its present form, Catholicism was still, in Hawthorne's thinking, synonymous with ecclesiastical despotism.[62] Protestantism, he felt, needed to be converted "into something positive," but apparently not into something as "positive" as Catholicism. His democratic heritage rebelled against the "despotic government" which "perhaps destroyed [a people's] . . . principle of cohesion, and crumbled them to atoms." [63] Throughout his tales and novels, there are frequent references to the "irresponsible dynasty of Holy Fathers" (*MF*, VI, 123), "papal despotism" (*MF*, VI, 133), "Popish Monarch[s]" and "Popish tyrant[s]" ("The Gray Champion," I, 21, 29), "priest-ridden Italy" (*MF*, VI, 307). And in a preparatory study for one of the novels of his last phase, *Dr. Grimshawe's Secret*, he mediated on how to make Mr. Braithwaite "a symbol of evil and wily designs." His decision was that this might best be achieved by sketching him as "Italianized throughout and Popishfied." [64]

6

Admittedly, therefore, Hawthorne found in Catholicism much that was admirable, much that Protestantism might well adopt for its own. But he was repelled by its authoritarianism, by the failure of its professed adherents to live up to what he conceived to be the precepts of their religion.

It is abundantly clear, from both his pro- and anti-Catholic comments, that Hawthorne made no attempt to get at the fundamental dogmas of the Catholic religion. Even a casual knowledge of the actual beliefs of Catholics would have kept him from saying that the attendants in the churches of Rome "do not hesitate to interfere with the great purposes for which their churches were built and decorated; hanging curtains, for instance, before all the celebrated pictures, or hiding them away in the sacristy, so that they cannot be seen without a fee." [65] That Catholic churches should have been erected for "the great purpose" of serving as ecclesiastical art galleries is a conception utterly without basis in fact. Yet it is, I believe, typical of Hawthorne's determination to judge Catholicism with his emotions rather than with his intellect. Had his approach been intellectual, he could not naively have rejected a code of faith and morals simply because certain of its adherents did not meet the requirements of that code.

Yet even with, or perhaps because of, this purely surface and emotional approach, Hawthorne found himself inescapably attracted to Catholicism, especially, as has already been pointed out, to its "institution" of the confessional. That feature in itself was sufficient to render his final judgment of Catholicism favorable rather than otherwise.

There is no evidence to indicate, however, that Hawthorne ever contemplated joining the Catholic Church. Rumors to that effect may, indeed, have been current during his protracted stay in Italy; but Ada Adeline Shepard, who accompanied the Hawthornes on their tour of the continent and was very closely associated with them during all that time, categorically denies that such a rumor has any foundation in fact. Writing to her family on August 6, 1858, she remarks:

Probably you will hear, before long, that the Hawthornes have become Catholics; but you must not place any faith in such a report, if it does prevail. It was rumored in Rome last winter; but it has not the slightest foundation.[66]

It would seem, then, that there is little value in Theodore Maynard's conjecture that Hawthorne "had a bad conscience regarding the Catholic Church." [67] Mr. Maynard contends that the New England novelist, though conscious of an obligation to join what he considered to be the true Church, deliberately refused to become a Catholic. Presumably his reasons for such a refusal would include an inordinate fear of the reaction his conversion might have on family and friends. Mr. Maynard implies that the tension thus set up in Hawthorne may well explain the literary sterility of the last phase.

This hypothesis, while ingenious, cannot be substantiated by the record of Hawthorne's thinking. Nathaniel Hawthorne did not know the basic dogmas of Catholicism; what is more, he had no inclination and made no effort to learn them. Various outward manifestations of that religion he came to understand and respect; others, equally surface, he found repulsive. Cognizant only of the outward shell of the Catholic Faith and absolutely immune to a knowledge of the underlying principles of that Faith, it seems somewhat unlikely that his last four years should have been filled with an inner turmoil directly ascribable to his deliberate refusal to accede to what he felt to be an obligation to join the Church. Such an urge, had it existed, would certainly have led him to initiate a closer study of the dogmas and history of the Catholic religion. There is no record of such an attempt.

Nor does the fact that his youngest daughter Rose later became a Catholic nun and founded a religious Sisterhood prove that Hawthorne himself was already so favorably disposed to Catholicism as to be on the verge of becoming a Catholic, had not his untimely death intervened. As for his literary failures after *The Marble Faun*, these can be accounted for in ways far less tenuous than the one suggested by Mr. Maynard. It is entirely probable, for example, that his failing health rendered creative activity no longer possible.

Nathaniel Hawthorne consistently referred to himself as purely and simply a Protestant.[68] But I believe Dr. Henry Arlin Turner does the New England novelist an injustice when he speaks of Hawthorne's "hatred for Catholicism and tyranny."[69] Hawthorne recognized Catholicism as one form of Christianity; he admitted that a great many people find their spiritual advantage in it, who would find none at all in our formless mode of worship."[70] But his final conclusion must have been that it was not for him. Hawthorne, in fact, should not be characterized as a man congenitally hostile to creeds and sects and denominations. He simply refused to commit himself to one rather than another, possibly because he could not resolve his doubts as to which sect was the right one.

This much is established. He was not a pagan. He was not a Catholic. He was a Protestant, though affiliated with no specific Protestant sect. For a delineation of the precise nature of his beliefs indicates a personal eclecticism that defies any attempt at easy classification.

NOTES

[1] For more detailed accounts of the religious turmoil in which Puritanism expired, consult Haroutunian, *op. cit.*; Cooke, *op. cit.*; William Warren Sweet, *Religion in Colonial America* (New York: Charles Scribner's Sons, 1942); Henry Bamford Parkes, "The Puritan Heresy," *Hound and Horn,* V (January-March, 1932), 165-190.

[2] Samuel T. Pickard, *Hawthorne's First Diary* (Boston and New York: Houghton, Mifflin and Company, 1897), p. 14.

[3] Stearns, *op. cit.*, p. 57, calls attention to an ode which the young Hawthorne "may have composed as early as his fifteenth year." One of its typical stanzas is the following:

> Then I have seen the storm disperse,
> And Mercy hush the whirlwind fierce,
> And all my soul in transport owned
> There is a God, in Heaven enthroned.

[4] Pearson, *op. cit.*, p. 88.

[5] Letter to Louisa Hawthorne, April 14, 1822.

[6] Yale University transcript of HM 11047 (Huntington Library MSS).

[7] Horatio Bridge, *Personal Recollections of Nathaniel Hawthorne* (New York: Harper and Brothers Publishers, 1893), p. 33.

[8] Pearson, *op. cit.*, pp. xxvii ff.

[9] Kesselring, *loc. cit.*, LIII (February, 1949), 58.

[10] John Cline, "Hawthorne and the Bible" (Unpublished Ph.D. dissertation, Department of English, Duke University, 1948), p. 32.

[11] *The American Notebooks,* p. 17.

[12] *Ibid.*, p. 46.

[13] *Ibid.*, p. 220.

[14] *The English Notebooks,* p. 432.

[15] Richard Henry Stoddard, *Recollections Personal and Literary,* ed. Ripley Hitchcock (New York: A. S. Barnes and Company, 1903), p. 121.

[16] *The American Notebooks,* p. 230.

[17] In a letter to his wife, dated April 14, 1844, he spoke of meeting Mr. Waterston quite accidentally, and much to his sorrow, since he "anticipated a great deal of bore and botheration." Fortunately, the clergyman "merely spoke a few words, and then left me. This is so unlike his deportment in times past, that I suspect the Celestial Rail Road must have given him a pique; and if so, I shall feel as if Providence had sufficiently rewarded me for that pious labor."

[18] *The American Notebooks,* p. 168.

[19] *Ibid.*, pp. 157 f.

[20] Letter to Sophia Peabody, April 13, 1841.

[21] Letter to Sophia Peabody, April 16, [1841].

[22] Letter to Epes Sargent, October 21, 1842; the magazine referred to is the short-lived (January to June, 1843) *Sargent's New Monthly Magazine of Literature, Fashion and the Fine Arts.*

23 *The English Notebooks*, p. 37.

24 *Ibid.*, p. 451.

25 *The American Notebooks*, p. 158.

26 *Ibid.*, p. 165.

27 *The French and Italian Notebooks*, II, 229.

28 *The English Notebooks*, p. 198.

29 *Ibid.*, p. 101.

30 *Ibid.*, p. 257.

31 Cf. *The American Notebooks*, p. 8; *The English Notebooks*, pp. 211, 386, for mention of his attendance at religious services. On other occasions, he attended for no other reason than to see what he could of the cathedrals in which the services were being conducted—cf. *Ibid.*, pp. 223, 541. Various entries state specifically that his wife attended, but not he: *The American Notebooks*, p. 169; *The English Notebooks*, pp. 46, 503.

32 *Ibid.*, p. 55.

33 Harold P. Miller, "Hawthorne Surveys His Contemporaries," *American Literature*, XII (May, 1940), 232.

34 *The French and Italian Notebooks*, III, 611.

35 *Ibid.*, III, 657. Cf. also *Ibid.*, II, 277; III, 671.

36 *Ibid.*, III, 694 f.

37 *Ibid.*, II, 358.

38 *Ibid.*, II, 228.

39 *Ibid.*, II, 229.

40 *Ibid.*, II, 114. Cf. also *Ibid.*, II, 73.

41 *Ibid.*, II, 9. Cf. also *Ibid.*, III, 732.

42 *Ibid.*, III, 572 f.

43 *Ibid.*, III, 573.

44 *Ibid.*, II, 114.

45 *Ibid.*, II, 73 f.

46 *Ibid.*, II, 74.

47 *Ibid.*, III, 574.

48 *Ibid.*, II, 74.

49 *Ibid.*, II, 110.

50 Cf. *The American Notebooks*, pp. 248, 266.

51 *The French and Italian Notebooks*, II, 110.

52 Quoted in Arlin Turner, *Hawthorne as Editor*, p. 58.

53 *The French and Italian Notebooks*, II, 114.

54 *Ibid.*, III, 574.

55 *Ibid.*, III, 441.

56 *Ibid.*, II, 327.

57 *Ibid.*, II, 391 f.

58 *Ibid.*, II, 491.

59 *The American Magazine of Useful and Entertaining Knowledge*, as quoted in Arlin Turner, *Hawthorne as Editor*, p. 175.

60 *The French and Italian Notebooks*, II, 302.

61 *Ibid.*, II, 125.

62 *Ibid.*, III, 695.

[63] *Ibid.,* III, 515.

[64] Edward Hutchins Davidson, *Hawthorne's Last Phase* (New Haven: Yale University Press, 1949), p. 56.

[65] *The French and Italian Notebooks,* II, 327 f.

[66] The Ada Shepard Letters, a type-script copy of which is available in the Yale University Library's Hawthorne Collection.

[67] Theodore Maynard, "The Hawthorne Year," *The Catholic World,* CLXVIII (January, 1949), 285.

[68] *The French and Italian Notebooks,* II, 141; II, 33.

[69] Henry Arlin Turner, "A Study of Hawthorne's Origins" (Unpublished Ph.D. dissertation, Department of English, University of Texas, 1934), p. 173.

[70] *The French and Italian Notebooks,* II, 73 f.

The secret of this strange mirth lay in the troubled state of his spirits, which, like the vexed ocean at midnight (if the simile be not too magnificent), tossed forth a mysterious brightness.

—*Fanshawe*, XI, 133.

V Summary and Corollaries

In the final year of his earthly life, on January 2, 1864, Nathaniel Hawthorne wrote his long-time friend, Henry Wadsworth Longfellow, that he had begun one more book, "but with no assurance of ever bringing it to an end. As is always the case, I have a notion that this last work would be my best, and full of wisdom about matters of life and death—and yet it will be no deadly disappointment if I am compelled to drop it."

Fifteen days later he penned a note to his publisher, James T. Fields:

You ought to be thankful that (like most other broken-down authors) I do not pester you with decrepit pages, and insist upon your accepting them as full of the old spirit and vigor. That trouble, perhaps, still awaits you, after I shall have reached a further stage of decay.

Seriously, my mind has, for the present, lost its temper and its fine edge, and I have an instinct that I had better keep quiet.

Five months later, Nathaniel Hawthorne was dead, the book which was to be "full of wisdom about matters of life and death" still unwritten. That this might have proved to be his best work, had he lived to complete it, no one will deny; but that it would have embodied thoughts "about matters of life and death" radically different from those previously incorporated into his novels and short stories is highly improbable. For the record shows that Hawthorne very early in his life evolved a theology that was personal to him, yet at the same time fundamentally Christian and, more often than not, decidedly orthodox.

On what foundations he erected this theological superstructure is a matter for conjecture. Like Theodore Parker,[1] he may have accepted the three "primal intuitions" laid in human nature itself: the instinctive intuition of the divine, the instinctive intuition of the just and right, the instinctive intuition of the immortal. Basing himself largely, though not exclusively, on these three "primal intuitions," he may have evolved the various concepts which underlie his allegorical representations of moral drama.

On the other hand, it seems more in accord with the foliations of his religious thinking to say that he accepted, without previous logical scrutiny, a set of dogmas founded partially on the Christian revelation and partially on reason; having accepted this initial core of belief, he then modified it to meet the exigencies of his own thought and experience.

2

Against the basic framework of Hawthorne's theology, certain obvious conclusions suggest themselves.

Nathaniel Hawthorne's theological thinking is Arminian rather than Calvinistic. In contrast to the recognized teachers of Puritanism, he insisted upon each individual's own role in the important business of working out his happiness. Unlike these same Puritan divines, who thought that the good of man consisted ultimately in glorifying God, Hawthorne believed that the glory of God was to be identified with the happiness of His creatures. Precisely what constituted this happiness

Hawthorne did not choose to define. He was willing to admit that man himself, a finite, limited being, could never be the judge of his own happiness. This was reserved to God alone, who, by devious ways incomprehensible to man, ordered everything so as to help each creature to realize his happiness. Man, therefore, needed a firm and childlike reliance upon the wisdom and goodness of God, a reliance that transcended all apparent indications that the plan and will of God either was not operative or was operating against man's best interests. To those who trust in God—and this was Hawthorne's belief—everything will come out all right in the end. But the end is not necessarily a large bank account and a mortgage-free mansion by the seashore; rather, it is nothing less than man's realization that, whatever the will of God in his behalf, in that will lies his peace and his happiness. With Dante he may well have said, *"E la sua volontate è nostra pace."*

Hawthorne's concern, therefore, lay primarily in the conflict arising from a divergence in man's point of view and God's point of view. When the former prevailed, when man insisted upon his own touchstones of happiness, the result was frustration, tension, sin; when man submitted his judgment to the long-range wisdom of God, then happiness would come "all unawares."

The keystone, then, of Hawthorne's theology is an unshakable belief in an inscrutable Providence; and it is from the vantage point of this belief that he reconciles man to the problem of evil.

The static character of Hawthorne's theological thinking is an established commonplace; Julian Hawthorne, in his *Memoirs,* makes it quite clear that, in his opinion, the early tales "contain Hawthorne's philosophy of life, speculations and conclusions upon matters vital to all mankind. They constitute . . . the corner-stone of his view of the problem of man, God, and the nature which is the medium between them." [2]   And while the New England novelist never wavered in his firm reliance upon God's providence, the record of his thinking shows that, in his later works, he was inclined to attribute to this providence an ever wider and more complex sphere of activity.   In 1843, for example, he expressed his conviction that "the bad habits and sinful propensities which have overrun the moral world" could not have any good in them whatsoever.[3]   In *The Marble Faun* he is willing to admit that the evil deeds of man may be "so beneficently handled by omniscience and omnipotence" (VI, 492) as to become the occasion of good.

The record shows, then, a gradual darkening of the shadows of gloom and despondency that lie beneath the crust of purely human happiness.   But the effect of this darkening serves only to accentuate the contrast between it and the "eternal beauty" that is deeper than the blackness.   The life of man, in other words, is to be regarded as constituted by three layers:

1. the outer shell of natural bliss;
2. the gloom and darkness and frustration beneath this outer layer;
3. the core of "eternal beauty," the operation of God's providence, at the very center of life.

Whatever development is to be found in Hawthorne's theological thought revolves about this second layer. For the most part it consists in deepening the shadows and the gloom; and in so far as he increases the darkness, so much the more does he accentuate the wisdom and mercy of God, who, whatever men may think to the contrary, does all things well.   For God's omniscience and omnipotence are in no way limited by man's failure to comprehend the full implication of such attributes.[4]

In fact, whereas the evil in the world has in every age been construed into an argument against a belief in an all-good and an all-wise God, Hawthorne would seem to have used the evil in men's lives as an argument in favor of God's existence. The darkness which made men doubt the light drove Hawthorne to the realization that they could never know darkness unless there was light. In a very true sense, therefore, Hawthorne came to God through his keen consciousness of moral and physical evil.

Yet a third general conclusion suggests itself in the light of this investigation into Hawthorne's theology. The New England novelist is at his artistic best in those tales in which he strives to penetrate beyond the layer of gloom and despondency to the eternal beauty beneath. The more pronounced the blackness, so much the greater his apprehension that he may never be able to thread his way through the blackness to the light beyond. Then, as he once wrote of Fanshawe, "the troubled state of his spirits . . . like the vexed ocean at midnight . . . [tosses] forth a mysterious brightness" (XI, 133). It is this "mysterious brightness" which is the touchstone of his finest tales.

Finally, Hawthorne has frequently enough been censored for a failure to systematize his theology. The charge stands. But there is an undeniable consistency in his theological approach, in his religious attitude. This consistency derives from his unceasing efforts to reconcile the incongruity of Divine Omnipotence and outraged, suffering humanity. In virtue of this pervading consistency, the theology of Nathaniel Hawthorne achieves a coherence which, while it may well elude the professional theologian, is inescapably manifest to any reader who realizes that mere literal meanings and logical exposition will never suffice to convey ineffable truth.

NOTES

[1] J. Weiss, *The Life and Correspondence of Theodore Parker* (New York: D. Appleton and Company, 1864), II, 454 f.

[2] *The Memoirs of Julian Hawthorne* (New York: The Macmillan Company, 1938), p. 214.

[3] *The American Notebooks,* p. 186.

[4] "The Hall of Fantasy," II, 207.

Index

A NOTE ON THE TYPE

IN WHICH THIS BOOK IS SET

This book is set in Times Roman, a Linotype face created by Stanley Morrison, world-famous typographical authority. Designed for the London *Times* which demanded a type face that should be clear and legible, precise but not mechanical, having a high letter but not condensed, of a "color" suitable for any paper or printing process, with character but not with annoying characteristics. Notice the clear, open characters of Times Roman. This is the secret of its clear printing on any paper, whether it be on the coarsest of newsprint or the finest coated paper. This book was composed and printed by the Wickersham Printing Company of Lancaster, Pa., and bound by Moore and Company of Baltimore. Typography and design by Howard N. King.